Journal of the Fantastic in the Arts

Volume 35 Number 3

I0172421

JFA

Journal of the Fantastic in the Arts
Volume 35/ Number 3

FAVIAN PRESS

A FAVIAN PRESS PAPERBACK

© Copyright 2024
JFA

The right of JFA to be identified as author of this work has been asserted in accordance with the Copyright, Designs and Patents Act 1988

All Rights Reserved

No reproduction, copy or transmission of the publication may be made without written permission. No paragraph of this publication may be reproduced, copied or transmitted save with the written permission of the publisher, or in accordance with the provisions of the Copyright Act 1956 (as amended).

Any person who does any unauthorised act in relation to this publication may be liable to criminal prosecution and civil claims for damages.

ISBN 978 1 78695 899 0

Published by Favian Press
an imprint of Fiction4All
www.fiction4all.com

This edition published 2025

Editors-in-Chief	Jude Wright *Managing*
	Cat Ashton *Production*
	Novella Brooks de Vita *Acquisitions and Reviews*
Senior Submissions and Reviews Editor	Farah Mendlesohn
Submissions Editor	Tedd Hawks
Peer Review Editor	Ida Yoshinaga
Copy Editor	Cat Ashton
Accessibility & Sensitivity Coordinator	Alexis Brooks de Vita
Regional Submissions, Accessibility, Sensitivity & Reviews Editors	Taryne Taylor
	Sang-Keun Yoo
Editor-at-Large	Dale Knickerbocker
Editorial Advisory Board	Michelle Anya Anjirbag Cristina Bacchilega Kyle William Bishop Jim Casey Ian Campbell Bodhisattva Chattopadhyay F. Brett Cox Mame Bougouma Diene Grace Dillon Tananarive Due

Neil Gaiman
John Garrison
Mads Haahr
Regina Hansen
Rachel Haywood
Kathryn Hume
Aaron Kashtan
Brooks Landon
Isiah Lavender III
Roger Luckhurst
Rob Maslen
Cheryl Morgan
James Morrow
Alec Nevala-Lee
Joy Sanchez-Taylor
Wole Talabi
Sherryl Vint
Gary K. Wolfe

COVER ART
"Untitled"
Nancy Hightower has taught Writing about Art at the University of Colorado, as well as Writing in the Art and Design Professions at the Fashion Institute of Technology. Her photography has been published in *Epiphany, The Evergreen Review, Cagibi Lit*, and elsewhere. Her prints can be found at https://nancyhigh.picfair.com/

GENERAL INQUIRIES
Inquiries and other editorial correspondence should be directed to journal@fantastic-arts.org.

SUBMISSIONS
Like the International Conference on the Fantastic in the Arts, *JFA* welcomes papers on all aspects of the fantastic in world literatures and media, as well as interdisciplinary approaches including African/Diaspora Studies, anthropology, area studies, critical game

studies, disability studies, future studies, gender studies, history, Indigenous studies, music, philosophy, political science, postcolonial studies, psychology, queer studies, religious studies, science and technology studies, and sociology. All papers are made available in English and fully refereed. The journal is indexed in the MLA Bibliography.

Submissions should contain a more in-depth discussion than a conference-length paper and demonstrate a grasp of current scholarship on the subject. The length of articles generally varies from 3,500-9,000 words and ranges from 15-35 pages.

All submissions are peer-reviewed in accordance with our peer review statement, the *Submission, Accessibility and Sensitivity Review Handbook*, and the BIPOC Anti-Racist Statement on Scholarly Reviewing Practices. If submissions are flagged at any point of the review process for the risk of promulgating potentially misrepresentative, stereotypical, ableist, or racist views, contributors will be asked to address these problems before the review process can continue.

Since the refereeing process is anonymous, the author's name should not appear anywhere on the text file itself, including the notes. No title page is needed. However, an abstract of 100-150 words must be inserted at the beginning of each submission, clearly stating what contribution the essay makes to the study of the fantastic.

Please ensure that all citations and the Works Cited entries are in current MLA style. Please do not use automatically generated notes; end notes (only) must be entered manually. A paper that doesn't meet our printing parameters can take many hours to adjust. To avoid needless changes and delays, it is best to use our guidelines from the start. For complete guidelines, please refer to the *Submission, Accessibility and Sensitivity Review Handbook* and the *JFA In-House Style Guide*. In case of conflicting instructions, defer to the *Submission, Accessibility and Sensitivity Review Handbook* and the *JFA In-House Style Guide*. Contributors are responsible for acquiring all permissions to quote and/or use illustrations that accompany their article, and for paying (or arranging to have their institutions pay) all usage fees, including copyright.

Due to the need to provide the journal in multiple formats, the journal does not currently publish images/illustrations in articles.

Scholarly articles should be directed to the *JFA*'s Acquisitions and Reviews team (under Editor-in-Chief Novella Brooks de Vita at jfa.acquisitions@fantastic-arts.org). Please send your anonymized submission to the Submissions Editor, Tedd Hawks, at journal@fantastic-arts.org and include "ATTN: JFA Article Submission" at the start of your subject line. Allow thirty days for confirmation of receipt before querying.

BOOK REVIEWS
JFA also publishes reviews of scholarly works addressing the fantastic, broadly construed. Reviews of fiction are limited to reissues of speculative works with new introductions and scholarly apparatuses, and speculative works with the potential to impact scholarship in the genre. Books and other media received are advertised on the IAFA discussion list (which can be subscribed to through the IAFA homepage at www.iafa.org), and IAFA members are encouraged to suggest titles for review.

To mail book copies for review and for queries or reviews of English-language publications, please contact the *JFA* at journal@fantastic-arts.org.

Contents

Creative Think Piece: Puddles are Portals

Nancy Hightower

FALL OF 2016 FEELS LIKE A CENTURY AGO, a *once upon a time* kind of beginning. I say this with certainty as I look at a photograph from that year. In it, my first-year students pose for an end of the semester picture. They are being silly and exuberant, cool and embarrassed all at the same time as only young people can be, full of hope despite the outcome of an election that would endanger their lives, with smiles that seemed to defy reality.

Two election cycles and a pandemic later left me revisiting that photo as more smiles disappeared with each semester, and with worry and exhaustion replacing the joy and excitement I saw before. At times, I can detect glimpses of something approaching gratitude, but when I ask them if they have fun, they shake their heads. If I follow up with what gives them joy, I might as well be asking what life is like on Mars.

My friends are no different. They are worried about job security and health insurance in a culture that promotes 24-hour news cycles and 60-hour work weeks. It's almost as if we are being trained to live on borrowed time. In their excellent essay, "Counterproductive Habits of Mind," David Rosenwasser and Jill

Stephen argue that we are often "somewhere else—especially if the activity we are doing is seen as boring or mundane" (n.p.). Rather than being fully present in the moment, we calculate what must be done in the next hour, later that evening, or by tomorrow. We replay the conversation we had yesterday, how the date went three days ago, or the presentation last week. In *A Swiftly Tilting Planet*, Charles Wallace is always being corrected to ask about the *when* they've traveled to instead of the *where*, and this might be a good question to ask ourselves. Humans aren't meant to time travel, and doing so in a capitalistic system where we are always on the clock racks up unfathomable debt by way of ill health, sleepless nights, missed deadlines, depression, anxiety, and a nameless dread that never quite goes away.

I have no easy answer on how to be more mindful at a point in the Zeitgeist when our attention is already frayed thin with only *what ifs* on the horizon. The authors of "Counterproductive Habits of Mind" remind us of David Lodge's thesis that art revitalizes the way we see the mundane through "defamiliarization" (Lodge 53; Rosenwasser and Stephen, n.p.), but what if it did more than that? What if art has the power to put us back in time, back in the *now*, where we can reconnect with wonder. My own artistic practice of taking photographs of New York City in puddle reflections demands a certain amount of both presence and wild abandon. Like Alice in Wonderland, I have to believe that even the smallest, muddiest puddle can show me a reflection that I can't even imagine.

This means I'm looking down and all around as opposed to straight ahead. I have circled a puddle many times, crouching beside it and then standing up to look at the surrounding buildings to see what scene might be forming. Sometimes I find other worlds, and sometimes, there's just really dirty water. Yet the practice of this art always produces joy and wonder and returns me to the right timeline. Could that be what was missing in my college classes?

When one thinks of *school*, one does not think *joy* or *whimsy* (unless we remember our kindergarten days when everything was new). I experimented with creating a radical defamiliarization of my classroom. I brought in tea lights and holiday lighting so that we didn't need the overhead lights on. I had two different machines that either produced a disco strobe lighting effect or the Northern Lights. I played disco music as they came in to find their seats. Was it harder for them to check their phones or having thirty tabs open on their computer? No, but were they more engaged? Yes, because art demands that we engage with it. Art returns us to this timeline.

2025 feels like it might be a terrifying year. As an adjunct instructor, my job is not secure. My housing in NYC is not secure. I will turn 55 in July, and my health insurance is contingent on whether I get enough courses. Will I still bring twinkle lights into my classrooms? I hope so, because we will need joy and wonder, along with community care, more than ever before. Rather than exhaust me, this kind of mindful presence increases my empathy, despite the large bag I carry to every class full of lights and food. One student said I reminded them of Mary Poppins, but true magic is created in community. I remember how before the pandemic, a small gang of first-year students would grab pizza after my class and encourage others to join, including the loner who sat in back. She was a passionate poet and scholar, and within a few years was listed as one of Time's *Women of the Year* for her role in being a climate change activist. My students are starlight.

Puddles are portals, which might explain why they lay hidden in plain sight. As children, we instinctively knew this truth and tried to jump into another world with gleeful anticipation. As adults, we view them as nuisance and a sign of bad drainage.

We forget that art is a bowing down. Art demands I give up my ego so that a city can show me the future of herself underwater. Ego is all about expecting the world as I want it to be. Art demands that I hunch over a puddle in the freezing rain, skirt wet and fingers numb to find a universe I never imagined. Art creates space for the world to tell the story of its joy and pain; it transforms the timeline to one of hope rooted in community. It reminds us that our daily planners, which propel us into anxious futures, must become a tesseract.

Works Cited

Carroll, Lewis. *Alice's Adventures in Wonderland*. London: Macmillan, 1865.

L'Engle, Madeleine. *A Swiftly Tilting Planet*. Farrar, Straus, and Giroux, 1978.

Lodge, David. *The Art of Fiction*. New York: Penguin, 1992

Rosenwasser, David, and Jill Stephen. "Counterproductive Habits of Mind." *Writing Analytically*, Cengage Learning, 2015. https://faculty.cengage.com/works/9780357793657

"The Connective Sinew Inside the Story": Interview with Steven Barnes, Guest of Honor

Steven Barnes,
Interviewed by Alexis Brooks de Vita

STEVEN BARNES: LET'S DO THIS.

JFA: Perfectly on time. Excellent. Thank you. So, Steven, welcome. Welcome back to VICFA.

Steven Barnes: Thank you.

JFA: And this time, I hope you don't mind if I tell you that you're actually helping us make history. You are our first African American man Guest of Honor.

Steven Barnes: I take that seriously.

JFA: And you are a brilliant and wonderful person to help us break down that barrier.

Steven Barnes: Oh! Thank you.

JFA: So, today, if I may, first I'll tell everybody your introduction, your summary bio. And then I want to hear from you. Is that okay?

Steven Barnes: You can ask me anything you want.

JFA: Thank you. So, welcome everyone. I'm Alexis Brooks de Vita, the BIPOC Caucus Rep, and you're in the Counter Space, the BIPOC Caucus's space for particularly innovative programming. And of course, all the spaces are innovative and challenging at the VICFA; we're building that reputation. And here is our Guest of

Honor, Steven Barnes. Steven Barnes is the *New York Times* bestselling author of over thirty novels of science fiction, horror, and suspense. The *Image, Endeavor*, and *Cable Ace* Award-winning author also writes for television, including *The Twilight Zone, Stargate SG One, Andromeda*, and an Emmy award-winning episode of *The Outer Limits*. Steven has also taught at UCLA, Seattle University and lectured at the Smithsonian Institute in Washington, DC. With his wife, British Fantasy Award-winning author Tananarive Due, he has created online courses in Afrofuturism, Black Horror and screenwriting. Steven was born in Los Angeles, California, and except for a decade in the Northwest, and three years in Atlanta, Georgia, has lived in that area all his life. Steve and Tananarive currently live with their son, Jason. Please join me in giving a very warm welcome to Guest of Honor Steven Barnes. We're thrilled to have you.

Steven Barnes: Thank you. Thank you.

JFA: So, I did not mean to cut you off. What were you saying?

Steven Barnes: Oh, shape this conversation in the way that it will be of the greatest value to people. As a matter of fact, just for the sake of fun, I will show you guys something. Boom. You see that house? That was Octavia E. Butler's house, where she lived on West Boulevard during the years that I knew her. We lived about half a mile away from each other, and we spent a lot of time talking about life, the universe, and everything, but also the responsibilities and stresses of being the only African American science fiction writers in the world for almost twenty years at that time. Things have changed massively since then, of course. But I'm happy, I'm comfortable with the place of breaking the ice, of being the first one to do something. It's kind of, you know, my thing. So, what is it that I can offer you and your people, please?

JFA: So, we're going to talk a lot about being this barrier-breaker. You have a fantastic short story that is in an award-winning anthology that I want to get to: that's "IRL." You have a lot of work that you've been doing. You were here with your wife when we were talking about *The Keeper,* an amazing graphic novel. What I do want to do right now though is take everybody back. You did bring up Octavia Butler. She was a Guest of Honor at the IAFA a couple of decades ago, and I am very cognizant, very aware that you are the first African American man invited as a Guest of Honor. I do want to say there are so many layers in considering these challenges. Yes, both of you were writing science fiction at a time when African Americans could not really expect to be published if they were writing science fiction; and yet, you broke down those barriers. You're published. You are multi-published: we just read your impressive bio. Talk about that. Talk about being that political, social thinker who embraces difference and uniqueness, and what was it about science fiction?

Steven Barnes: Well, first of all, I've never considered myself to be very political. I'm very philosophical. To me, the difference is that philosophy is asking what is true. Politics is asking: how can we win? How can we organize groups of people to accomplish something? But I recognize it's a valuable thing, a necessary thing. It's not my thing. You know, they say that politics is war carried through by other means. War is politics extended by other means. I forget which. I'm thinking they also say that the first casualty of war is innocence or truth. To the degree that these are very similar, you know, politics is nasty, but it's not as nasty as throwing a grenade into somebody's bedroom. So, it's preferable to that. But the question of what is true is often the casualty. The question of kindness is often anathema. I mean I've lost friends for encouraging people to be kind and honest, according to the three gates in Sufism. So, they were very politicized. So, I've always been interested in what is true. And if I were to tie this back with my own history, I guess I'd say that it's reasonable that the more time you spend in fantasy and science fiction, the less likely you are to be totally happy with your life. You know that you're looking for another win, you're looking for another way to look at things, you're looking for an escape. I think that that's not unfair. I definitely am including myself in that category. So, as a kid, was I looking for other worlds? Other ways to look at things? Other answers? Absolutely, and to some degree, that isn't different from my White friends of my same age or my Asian friends of my same age, but I do think that the fact of my ethnicity was an additional spur there. Asking: why? You know, there are two basic questions in art: who are you, and what is true? Those are the same basic questions you have in philosophy: "Who am I? What is true?" And I've heard at least one reasonable speculation that the entire process of enlightenment per se could be written on the back of a postage stamp, in terms of you writing down those questions: who am I and what is true?

You keep digging into the answers to those questions until you run out of answers. And the estimation is that if you spend an hour a day doing this, in about two years, you could get through everything that your ego has created to mask reality, to define yourself. You would begin to unravel that ego cocoon, and you would be dealing with reality in a much more direct fashion. The concept of enlightenment is really connected to the question of being awake as opposed to asleep: to not simply believe the things that you're told about reality, and that, for good or ill, has been a real interest of mine, even before I knew that that was an interest, even before I knew that I was not what the world said I was. I knew that for a fact. But then that begged the next question: if I'm not that, if I'm not that thing, what am I?

I think that everybody eventually begins asking those questions. It's possible that I just started asking them a little earlier than most, which is not necessarily a good thing. It's not necessarily a happy thing. I would prefer to have kept illusions for a while longer. I would have preferred to believe that the world was a safe place: that the world saw me and would nurture me and would love me and support me. I wish I could have believed that, but I didn't. I think that the advantage I have is that I don't believe in talent. It's not that I don't think it exists purely, but I think it's not a useful concept. I've never heard anybody say I made it because of talent. The only ways I hear people talk about talent is "I didn't try it because I didn't have the talent." That person over there had talent. But I didn't, and I could not afford to leave anything in the locker room. I could not afford to not succeed. I had a belief that the world would grind me up and spit me out, if I did not succeed.

And so, a lot of my emphasis over most of my life was: how the hell do I do this? If my goal is to do something that I've never seen anybody else do that literally everybody tells me I can't do, what do I do? How do I do this? So, I would say that if I have a skill, if there's one thing about me, that I believe, it's connected to that question of is there any such thing as talent. If there is such a thing as talent, I think that it is the capacity to focus on one thing until you figure it out. Give me somebody who's got that, who is teachable, who is willing to follow what a mentor says. And I feel like I can make them a success in almost anything. Because that's all I've ever seen. Anytime I see somebody who's better than me at something, I see that they spend more time and energy.

Octavia, for instance, was a better writer than me, and she deserved to be a better writer than me. She put more of herself into it. You know, the world isn't unfair in that sense. So, in that sense, the one advantage that I seem to have is I'm too stupid to know when to quit. I just won't quit. You can kill me, but you cannot stop me. I mean, it took me twenty-three years to earn my first black belt. Because I was dealing with so much fear and confusion. So, to the question of being a writer: in some ways, once I realized that I would rather lose, I would rather have failed at being a writer than succeeded in anything else. And once I realized that, then it wasn't even a matter of "Can I succeed?" It was a matter of: how do I stay on this path and do my very best and give it everything I have and get the best chance? And then, if I give it everything, and I still don't make it, I can live with that. But if, at the end of my life, if, at the moment of death, I had an epiphany, and I saw that I could have been anything I wanted if I just had the courage to keep going, that would be horrifying. If, at the moment of death, I saw that my goals have been larger than my ability, I'd laugh.

It's like, "Oh well. I still had a hell of a ride." So, I was in one of those "burn your boats" positions: all or nothing positions. And from there, it was: write; learn; try to understand the game as much as possible. Try to clarify my own emotions so that I can wake up every day and have enthusiasm for what I'm doing. I mean, it's like can I gin up my enthusiasm for what I'm doing, day after day after day, no matter what happens? If you can do that, if you design your days so that the steps you take towards the goal are themselves beautiful things, that the reward itself is living your life one day at a time, in alignment with your own heart. It's up to the world to tell me how good I am or I'm not, according to what they think. I don't know whether or not I'll get to the next level, or whatever. My job is to live these days with integrity, and to do that in such a way that, if there is a chance for me to reach my goals, I've done the best I could to do that. Finding the ways to look at life and my career that enabled me, every day, to do the best I could, and enjoy my life, I mean, that was as much as I could do, as far as I could go. And I had to find ways to control my emotions because otherwise, you know, depression and, oh my god, artists get their guts kicked out.

Everybody knows that. It's horrible. You're trying to make a living doing something that everybody would do for free. How in the world are you supposed to make a living doing what everybody in the world wants to do? I mean, when you were a kid, you dance in the living room, and everybody thinks, oh you're so cute and they throw you dimes, and there's a part of us that never grows up from that place. "Aren't I cute? Aren't I wonderful? Give me your money." So, it's not easy, but life isn't easy. I'm asking the universe to let me spend my life doing something that I love, and I am so grateful that I've been able to do as much of that as I have. I've been extraordinarily fortunate. You know, I thank my mentors and the people who helped me along the way so much. Every day you wake up in the morning, and I forget who it was that said you wake up in the morning, and you take your little bit of talent, and you push it all into one corner, and you go to work on it. It's like that. I wake up every morning and it's like, what do I need to do today? Why am I getting out of bed? I have to take care of my family. I have to do this. I have to feed the cats. I have to be a good example for my son. I have to love my wife whose career is blowing up right now, and she really needs to know that her husband is right there, the wind beneath her wings: you go, girl; you soar as far as you can, as fast, but that also means I have to control some of my own ego stuff. You don't think there's a part of me that says, "I didn't get that review in the *New York Times*. I didn't get that review in the *Washington Post*; waah! What's wrong with me?" This is just the stuff, it's just what you have to deal with. And I feel blessed. Life has been very, very good to me, all things considered.

JFA: I am going to perhaps throw a little bit of a monkey wrench in there.

Steven Barnes: Oh. Do your best. Try. Bring it on. Come on.

JFA: But I am also from Los Angeles. I was also born and raised most of my life in Los Angeles. Not all of it, because when I was old enough to be married and have my first child, I realized I had to leave. And when I've gone back, I keep hearing people say, "Oh, Los Angeles has changed." And it wasn't until one of my daughters, my daughter and her husband, my son-in-law, took me to Los Angeles a year ago now, that I understood why people were saying it's changed. Where I was born, Watts, and where I was babysat by my aunt in South Central, these are no longer miles and miles of African American homes. Where my wealthiest friends lived in Baldwin Hills, these are no longer African American enclaves. And I only recently saw some statistics that Los Angeles is now, what, 5% African Americans? So, when I read your bio, and I read that you were born and raised and stayed there, I thought, "You saw that transition. You saw it."

Steven Barnes: Not the whole. I didn't stay here the whole time. I spent ten years in the Northwest and three years in Atlanta.

JFA: Not the whole. I read it. That's understandable. But excavating reality, rejecting stereotypes. I've taken some notes of some of your words. And this need to understand yourself and get up every day, and focus and build that enthusiasm from scratch, to clarify your emotions and decide what it is that you must do, right, to recognize yourself, to accept yourself? What you'd rather fail at, than succeed at something that would not have defined you to yourself? Then I could understand: this is the boy who grew to be the man who could stay when a city whose police force, whose systemic approach, was America's secret. You know, that, no, racism is not a Southern phenomenon. Racism is not.

Steven Barnes: It's not exclusively. I do think that it is more. I think it is more a Southern phenomenon. It's like every section of the country would have its own sins.

JFA: It has its own way.

Steven Barnes: You know, but you can get it everywhere because it's a human thing. It's the more toxic aspect of tribalism. And everyone's tribal. Tribalism is just, you know, babies have that: "My daddy is the strongest. My mom is the prettiest. My dog is the smartest." Transfer that to tribes of people, and it can get ugly.

JFA: So, with that, what I want to say is that some of what you have said is, I think, clearly delineated in that short story I told you that we would get to talk about. Right? You've written many brilliant things. But because of the subject of the conference, I do have to say that one of the most extraordinary short stories I've ever read that has to do with this subject of artificial intelligence is your gaming story. You have a young man who is in a very dystopian Los Angelesian society who disapproves of his father's choices. Who disapproves of his choices, and yet they're alone. This young man and his father who has protected him and taken care of him live with the ghost of the mother who has been lost. And in this incredibly intense environment, you introduce the fact that this young man has a gaming skill, and that his father is in danger in the real world, based on these competitions in the gaming world.

Steven Barnes: Yeah.

JFA: And it is so powerfully vivid that this brilliant young man realizes that he is going to have to save his father by taking the most extraordinary risks that he has ever taken: he's going to have to outthink the virtual gangs. He's going to have to do what no one can expect, in order to achieve that protection of the father.

Steven Barnes: I need to hire you as my marketing agent.

JFA [laughs]: You should. You should, and you could because this story is so full. It's a short story, yet the emotional depths. . . . The relationships, the resentments, what can't be said, what can't be explored, it's all so realistic.

Steven Barnes: Oh, thank you.

JFA: And living in this virtual world is so convincing, and the strategizing and his posse that is trying to come together and support him is so intense that I did think that you took growing up as an African American boy into an African American man in Los Angeles to the limits of sci-fi writing, It's brilliant, and anyone who wants to understand that sense of being embattled, that sense of being under the gun, under a microscope, of having to have invented a full other self, and who has invented that other self to survive, can read "IRL" and get that visceral experience.

Steven Barnes: Thank you.

JFA: It's a work of incredible achievement. So, I do want you to talk about what you were aiming for with that story.

Steven Barnes: Okay, I can do that. I mean, first of all, I'd like to say, you know, thank you because I don't take myself very seriously, as you can probably tell, but I take the work very seriously. I take the martial arts very seriously. I take my family very seriously. Those are really the only three things in the world I care about. So, when you say that something communicated to you, I take that seriously, and I thank you so much for communicating that. It means a lot. When I start any story—I mean I can talk about the process of writing, and somewhere in here, the question of what I was trying to do will come out. First, if I was trying to write a good story, or somebody says we'd like you to write a story, but I don't remember whether or not the thematics in that story were suggested. Let's say it wasn't. I've been experimenting with some ideas for a novel, and one of the things that I like to do is to pull an idea out and say let me write a story about this, let me solidify my IP. Let me kind of claim this universe. This is a universe in which certain things happen, certain things are true. And so, there it was: I wanted to play with an idea. So, that would be where I kind of started, and the idea had to do with virtual space, and the way people are getting lost in virtual space. Was it informed?

I don't think race had much to do with it, but I can tell you that my sense of having grown up without my father had a lot to do with it. The question of what the father-son bond is had a lot to do with it. That's something that has bedeviled me and concerned me a lot, you know, for many, many years. So, as I wrote this story, if there's a situation . . . . You can write a story two different ways. You can come up with a situation, or you can come up with a character. Those are the two basic ways. The character moves in the world. There is a situation. And the plot of a story is what a specific character does in that situation.

So, if you have Clint Eastwood standing in line at a 7/11, and there's a robbery, you know that situation comes out one particular way. If Kevin Hart is there with his girlfriend, that situation is going to come out another way. So, the plot is different. By moving back and forth between "What is the situation? Who would be the perfect person to look at the situation through?" or "Who is a character that I want to play with, and what would be the situation that would test that character?" you go back and forth between those things. And in the process of moving back and forth between "What's the situation and who's experiencing it?" and "Who's the character and what do they need to move to the next level of their lives that will test them fully, in terms of that hero's journey aspect?" What is the hero's journey details a movement from one level of life to another. Characters in broad stories, in mythic stories, are generally moving from one entire aspect of life to another. But there're also literary stories in which characters are moving around inside the same level. Oftentimes they will be confronted with a challenge and won't accept it. And so, the story is really kind of quiet.

It's existential despair. You know, the person who knows that they need to make a move, they need to get out of a marriage, they need to ask for a raise, they need to try to get a job. They need to do this, they need to do that, and they can't get themselves to do it because they're trapped by their own emotions. I like stories where people take action. Okay, that's just my personal preference. Nothing against the other kinds of stories. So, in that story, what I'm going to look for is: "What, what is the inertia? What is that psychological inertia, the thing that makes the person want to stay in a particular position, and then how can I give them enough pain? Or promise them enough pleasure to force them to make a decision?" In this particular case, it was this kid who is totally locked into the fantasy world, the virtual world, and he is forced to deal with the real world because even though he has a terrible relationship with his father, underneath all that, he loves his father. Of course, he does. Of course, he does. So, the story, a good story—often, maybe usually—is about the moment at which someone changes.

You might want to use the Aristotelian unity of time: it takes place within twenty-four hours. Not a bad idea. You start as close to the change as possible. That still gives your audience enough context to be able to feel what is happening. Once I have this situation, I have some basic notions of the beats of the situation, so I will create a series, maybe a set of three by five cards, and I'll kind of say, "Well, what is 'IRL' about?" I don't even know that I knew the title, initially. Well, there's this guy, and he does something, and it gets his dad into trouble because he makes an enemy, and the guy attacks him in the real world, so he has to cope with this in the virtual world. You know, thinking out kind of the pieces, the big chunks. It's totally inelegant. But that phase of writing is like dragging marble up from a quarry. Okay, you drag the big pieces of emotion, the big events up. It doesn't matter how ugly they look, and this process is very ugly. There's no grace to it. An awful lot of writers make the mistake of thinking that their first draft is supposed to look like somebody else's final draft. That is a lethal error. My attitude is your first drafts are supposed to suck. Your first drafts are supposed to be awful. And not only that, but you will go through—[laughs].

I don't know if you can see this. Can you see this? I drew this at another time, but it's still applicable. So, this is the sun. This is the Earth. These are the rays of the sun. So, when you start writing a story, you're right here. You're in the heat of the rays of the sun, and you're feeling, "Wow, this is going to be a terrific idea, this is going to be wonderful, and everybody is going to love it; it is going to move my career to the next level, you know; it's going to free the slaves, and all kinds of stuff like that. So, you begin to circumnavigate the globe. You go around the globe; you're orbiting the globe as you do your work. As you write, you put one word in front of the other, one sentence in front of another, one paragraph in front of another, and what inevitably happens is, at some point, you get to the point where you're in the penumbra. You are in the shadow.

You're not getting the heat or the light of the sun anymore. And at this point, it is terrifying. It feels like this isn't working. It has never worked. I don't see it. You know: the only reason I've had a career is because of affirmative action. Everything in the world you can think of comes into your head. And what gets you through at that point is discipline. And what gets you through it at that point is your understanding that this is the pattern of creativity. I have been through the dark night of the soul, which would be the hero's journey way of saying this. Countless times on countless projects. It happens every single time. It's never any more comfortable. But it's a little bit like if you run, or you bicycle, you get tired and tired and then you get a second wind. So, the first few times that you discover that, it's kind of a surprise. Oh, I feel bad, bad, bad; and then I feel good. The same thing is true at this because if I am willing to exert the discipline to keep going, eventually, I emerge out on the other side. And when that happens, when I have a first draft of the whole thing, that's very rough. But now I'm looking at it, instead of the story being behind my eyes. It's in front of my eyes. I can say, "Oh, this is kind of the story."

Now I start looking for thematic elements. I start looking for moments of truth. I start looking for the connective sinew inside the story. What does this character really want? What's the gap between what they said and what they meant? What is this? What is this? How is this? And if I keep just every day doing the work, eventually thematic threads will begin to emerge, psychological reality begins to emerge, ways to do the plot in different ways, you know, to start masking the strings, the puppet strings so that people forget the puppet strings and now they're just looking at the puppet. I mean, we know that it's just a puppet show, but if it's done properly, you forget the strings and you're thinking about the drama. We know that books are just ink on paper. But if we hook the emotions in the right way, people will go into their minds, find the emotions that are triggered, get into a flow there, and suddenly they're not reading ink, they're not looking at ink on paper, anymore. They're in a world. The same thing is true with movies and books. How do I hook you by creating a world you believe in, so that you say, wow, let's see some people move through this world? Or by creating a character you believe in, who has concerns that are like yours, and if at the core of it, it's an intellectual idea, like virtual reality, then I have to anchor that to an emotional reality, like: "I want my relationship with my father." If I can make you believe in this world, and make you believe that he wants to heal his relationship with his father, now I've got you. You've swallowed the hook. If you've ever gotten up at two o'clock in the morning to drink the glass of water, you turn on the television while you're sitting bleary-eyed on the couch, and something comes on television, and in five minutes, you're hooked. It's like, damn it, I can't go back to sleep. I have to see how this works out. I have to see what happens here. That's the thing that is the magic that writers try to go for, the creation of a world; it's not our world. The creation of people. I mean, Hamlet may be the most complex character all of fiction, but he isn't a thousandth as complex as a real human being.

But we try to create imitations of real human beings sufficiently that we can identify with what they want. They want to survive. They want sex. They want power. They want love. They want self-expression. They want to understand the world, or they want to die. You know, with courage. Something basic that we understand is used to enliven a character that starts out as no more than a stick figure. You're just pushing them from one place to another. But if you keep doing that, eventually that character will begin to talk to you about their world, about what they want, and now, now you've got a game. Now it's happening. Now it's magic; and that moment right there is one of the moments that all artists look for: the point where the artwork starts coming to life for you and tells you what you need to do. That's really what Stephen King refers to as the boys in the basement. So w hat that is really about is "Who am I? Why do people get lost in the virtual world? What is it that we're trying to do with our technology? How does this, how does our technology, express what it is that we are? And then, what is true? What is the world? What is the difference between living in the real world and living in the virtual world?" What are the things I was saying there? Is it his friends, even his friends who ended up helping him were virtual friends. His father was real, flesh and blood. And at some level, he got it. He woke up. So, the story then is about the moment he steps out of childhood into adulthood, that he awakens to what is real in the world. And, you know, so it starts. Just let me write a story, and it goes through these different stages. I can go into more like that, but as you probably notice, I can talk at any length about a new subject. So, be careful what you ask me. I hope that that answered your question.

JFA: Thank you, Steven, you did, and it's fascinating because I can hear in your description what you must have gone through and I noticed that you never said, in terms of hitting a taboo. Right? There is a lot about his contempt for his father, his hostility toward his father. And frankly it gets frightening, you know, for anyone who is looking at how alone these two are together, and it becomes dangerous.

Steven Barnes: Yes. Yes.

JFA: Right? That this son resents his father so much, and it doesn't matter if you as an adult outside the story can come up with reasons because the story is relentless, the story is moving on.

Steven Barnes: Yeah, they need each other to survive. But they have a hard time reaching out and connecting with each other, which creates enormous risk.

JFA: Yeah.

Steven Barnes: That goes into questions like "What is love, and why does love evolve?"

JFA: Exactly.

Steven Barnes: What is family? What do we actually need in the world, as opposed to what we want? How do we use entertainment to numb ourselves from the emptiness inside us? You know, if you strive to make the world real and the people real, then your unconscious mind will find ways to connect these things. And people will say things that you never considered. I can't put all the things in the story that an intelligent reader will find. If I do the story right, they're going to see things that I never thought of. And that's the way it works. And that's the risk of course as well as the benefit because you're kind of standing there naked. I mean, I do the best I can; I really care about the work. But inevitably, no matter what I do, it's not reality. You know, it's not, it can't be, perfect. I'm going to forget something. It's like those houses at Universal City. You know, the psycho house looks great from the front, but you step around the back, and there's nothing there. Ultimately, stories can be a lot like that. They look really great if I keep you in one position where your vision, your peripheral vision, doesn't catch any of the tricks that I used to make it feel like this is all happening. You always have to control point of view. You don't want people walking around behind the psycho house looking at the girders and stuff. You know, people say stories aren't finished. They escape. There's a lot of that. There's always more to be done, always more to be done, but at some point you hope that you've done enough there that a reader will go through a set of emotions and feel something that was worth their time. If they do that, then I earned my money.

JFA: So, Steve, it's like this conversation. You are speaking sincerely, you're speaking with vulnerability, you're speaking with tremendous humility, and what you're doing is you're generating other people's spontaneous emotions in response. We can all think about our vulnerabilities. We can all think about times that we tried so hard and we gave it absolutely everything and did not understand why it was taken the way it was. And I do want to ask you about that because you talked about, you know, there's inspiration, and you're in the sunlight, and then you're working and you're working and you're traveling through the cycle, and you hit the penumbra, and all is darkness and cold and loss. And you did talk about that it is discipline that gets you through. You must be self-disciplined, and that's life, but that's definitely art. And, therefore, I did want to ask you to talk with us a little bit about that. I mean, since you have come right to that point, in making us face the fact that there is a way to get through the shadow. Then discuss that. What about when the shadow says you can't write about this? What about the shadow that says, "This is not the kind of thing that anybody wants." What about, you know, if the shadow says, "But I can find all these grammatical errors," and instead you say, "Yes, but I'm trying to put it on paper today."

Steven Barnes: Okay, so let's kind of go with that a little bit. Let's work backwards from my ultimate intent. My ultimate intent is not to be excellent. My ultimate intent is to be masterful. Okay, I figure if I'm going to spend my life doing this, why should I settle for anything less than being a master? Now, the question then comes to: what is a master? You know, how can you say something like that? There's a guy named George Leonard who was the men's fitness columnist for *Esquire* magazine who wrote a book on mastery, and he said something very interesting. He said the average person—he was an Aikido master as well as a bunch of other things—he said the average person never becomes really good at anything because they can't handle the fallow periods. They can't handle the periods when they're working, and it doesn't seem like anything is happening. It's a lot like putting a souffle in the oven, or a seed in the soil. You don't see anything happening, but there's a lot going on under the surface that finally breaks through. I thought that's very interesting, but then I also asked the greatest master that I know, who I know as a personal friend, and who would be my primary Karate instructor, Steve Muhammad, who I've known for forty years, more than forty years. He is above the level of grandmaster. He can promote people to grandmaster. I'm a grandmaster within his system. And I asked him once, I said, what is mastery? And he's a very simply spoken man, so I'm going to rephrase what he said. But roughly it was: "When you can create spontaneously under pressure, you're a master."

Now, I took what these two people said, and I combined them, and I have the following attitude. Mastery is a verb, not a noun. It's a vector, not a position. Once you have learned the basics of your craft to the level of unconscious competence, such that you can create spontaneously under pressure, you are on the path of mastery as much as anyone else has ever been on that path, even if they are horizons distant from you.

And all there is, is the path. I've had three-hour private lessons with a man who might be the greatest martial arts instructor who ever lived. And he's a very simple man. And what I notice about him and other masters is they're always learning. They're always doing, and they're always teaching. In other words, they're in the midst of a process of being. They're not outside looking at it. So, people outside looking at it say, "Well, you're a master." Oh, you don't think you have anything to learn? Masters laugh at that notion. They're just students who didn't quit. That's all they are.

So, when I look at this stuff, then I have to ask myself, well how do you become a master of writing because I wanted mastery in three different areas. I wanted writing, I wanted martial arts and I wanted a family to love. Okay? And I believe that mastery is totally within human capacity. How ridiculous would it be if you could work your entire life, put everything you have into something, but no, you can't be a master? Are you kidding me? That's not what the term was supposed to mean. Okay?

It's not perfection unless perfection once again is a verb: the process of becoming more perfect. That makes sense to me: the process of mastery. That makes sense to me. But there is no endpoint. So, people who say, well, we can't get there, if there is no endpoint. People who say well, we can't get there, are just denying themselves the pleasure, and they're doing something else. They're cheating the new students. I remember many years ago when I was going to an Indonesian martial arts workshop. It's like we used to meet at seven o'clock in the morning, and then afterwards we would go to breakfast. I'm sitting at breakfast, and there are other students there. And one of them was a woman who was a black belt in something or other, and I was complaining about my performance: "Oh, I messed up this, I didn't do this one, I didn't do that right; damn it! Damn," and she looked at me, and she said, "Steve, shut up." She said, "If someone at your level isn't happy with their performance, how are the rest of us supposed to feel?" And, I realized at that moment that it was an odd kind of twisted ego, to constantly put myself down. Was I not then saying that my teachers were no good? I have no more right to say that I am not a grandmaster than I would have to promote myself to Black Belt. That's not up to me. That's up to the people I've trusted to create a standard and create a path for me to work on. And, at some point, they say, "Oh yes, you have the qualities that I was looking for."

So, if my intent was to become a master of writing, then you have to ask yourself the question, "Well, what is the price that you pay?" And if you listen to enough writers talking, one of the things that is very clear is one of the costs is you will fight your demons every day. You will fight your demons every day. And, if you know that's the case, and your commitment is to make it through, to be the best you can be, then you have to say, "What am I going to do when the demons come to call?" And if you look at the hero's journey, the dark night of the soul is inevitably there. It's simply part of the process of going from one level to the next. It's even physiological. You know, if you go to the gym, you push the weights until you reach muscle failure. That's how your brain knows to put resources into making you stronger because there is some challenge. You reach the limit of your capacity, so it says okay, we'll take some of your limited resources, and we'll put it over here.

What's the path through the dark matter of the soul? According to the hero's journey, it is the leap of faith. Faith is always one of three things: faith in yourself. Faith in your companions. Or faith in a higher power. So, when I wake up, and I'm working on a *Star Wars* novel right now, and it's due in fifty-six days, and if you don't think I can feel that pressure, I can feel those demons. But I know a few things. One of them is, I've been here before. This has happened countless times before. I'm going to be afraid because I care. Another is that I have the resources to know one of the secrets that is taught to fairly high-level meditators. That secret is: you are not the voices in your head. You are the one listening to the voices. There are entire schools of meditation. They're all about inquiring into who is it that listens. Who was the listener? Who was the observer? You cannot observe the observer. The instant you observe the observer, you've just created another observer position, and now the question is who is that?

So, when those voices say, "I cannot," I don't have to believe them. I don't have to associate with them. I know they're not me. I know that they're just, you know, they're there; maybe they're trying to protect me, maybe they're trying to hurt me, but they're not me. And if they're not me, then I have the ability to say, "Should I listen to it?" And what it comes down to is always, "What are my commitments?" You set yourself up in life so that you know what you need to do because you study the path of masters who have done it before you. So, I need to write every day, and I need to send my stuff in, and I need to read ten times as much as I write. You figure out what the path is, and then, every day, you walk that path. Every day, it's just chop wood, carry water, and all the demons will come up and the wolves will come out with this and this, but ultimately it comes down to one of the most important questions: "Can you keep your word to yourself or can't you? Can you keep your word to yourself?"

Because if you can keep your word to yourself, then it doesn't matter how you feel. It doesn't matter what anybody else says. It doesn't matter what's going on in your head. Do you or don't you keep your word? If you break it down that far, then you've got one thing. Maybe two things. You have a couple things to know. One is, "What is your intent?" And the other is, "Can I keep my word?" If there is one thing as Jack Palance said in *Russler's Roundup* or whatever that movie was, "You can work on just keeping your word." You understand that if I can keep my word, I can accomplish anything that I'm capable of. And ultimately, I think the secret to that is you don't give your word over things you're not willing to die for. And it's not that I'm willing to die for a story. Or for a *Star Wars* book. But this is the path of my life, and ultimately, I'm giving the hours and the energy that I give there; that is my life. I mean if every time you got a paycheck, you had to cut a joint off one of your fingers, you'd understand what you're exchanging for the money that you get. I am giving my life for this. I did bet my life on this. This is who I am. This is what I do.

So, every day, it's asking who am I? I'm the guy who gets up and does this shit. Okay, my wife and I have this thing when we get hit with a big challenge, you know: Hollywood wants to do this, they want to do this, want to throw a lot of money at us, or they want us to do this, and it gets scary. We look at each other, and we say, "We are that bitch." That's literally what we say. It's like we're the ones who can do this. We are a hunting pair. She is a lioness. I am a lion, and we are hunting for our family. And we will kill anything that gets in our way as long as that's an ethical situation. Okay. And if you're willing to kill what gets in your way, then it becomes easier to kill your own ego. Your ego will get in your way. Awareness of self is the greatest hindrance to physical action, something that Bruce Lee said. It's also a hindrance to writing or doing the arts or making love. Those things that are that primary. Creative expression. If you don't lose yourself, you're not doing it right. You know, a book that you read and you're constantly aware of the room wasn't a very good book. The books that are good, you fall through the page in the book. The sex that is good, you can't even remember your name afterwards. A really good workout, you know, it's like you just went pure animal on that heavy bag or whatever it is. We're looking for the flow, the flow state, which is the doorway to the highest state of mind that is still purely practical. The flow state leads to non-dualistic thought; non- dualistic thought is sort of the end of the road. When it comes to useful thought, non-dualistic thinkers, they nail them to crosses.

You know, you're going to get assassinated. You talk about that stuff to the wrong people, that is very threatening to the ego. So, all the things you're talking about are the obstacles between you and being in the flow state and getting it done. If your commitment is to getting it done because if you get it done, you get to stay on the path of mastery, then you get familiar with the demons. You read stories about great artists and great thinkers and you say, "Oh, all of them have gone through this." This is just the way it is. There's that demon, and to a certain degree, when those demons pop up, it means you're doing your work: "Oh, there's a demon." If the demons never pop up, you're not pushing yourself.

I remember a guy—one of the first book signings I ever did—an older guy showed up at the book signing. He gave me his business card, and the business card said freelance hack and literary mechanic. And he was dead of alcoholism within a year. Art is a high wire act. Art is self-expression. If you try to create a work of art, and when you start it, you already know you can do it, you're not pushing yourself; you should be a little bit afraid. And to that degree, when the demons pop up, it means—Ah!—I'm on the path. The demons are back. So, they're actually a good thing. I like my demons.

JFA: That's a very positive note. I'm going to pause a second and check to see if there are questions because I see that people have put some things in chat.

Steven Barnes: Great!

Algorithmic Care in the Age of Machine Learning: Plenary Address by Distinguished Scholar Jennifer Rhee

Jennifer Rhee

Hosted by Andrew Erickson

I'm very honored to be speaking at VICFA, and I look forward to attending some exciting panels and being part of this larger conversation on AI, algorithms, automata, and art. In my previous research, I examined the racialized and gendered conceptions of the human that structured various AI systems and their automation of different forms of labor. I also highlighted how connections between these technological systems and speculative fiction and artworks have been shaping AI imaginaries. For example, in my book *The Robotic Imaginary*, I analyzed early conversational AI systems and their replication of the racialized and gendered hierarchies of care labor; a then-revolutionary approach to robotics called embodied and situated robotics, which extended the broader devaluation of domestic labor while reproducing historic racialized hierarchies within this gendered mode of labor; I also looked at affective or sociable robotics, which is based on a theory of emotions that universalizes white, Western, and ableist norms around the appropriate emotional responses and the appropriate corresponding facial expressions within any given situation; racialized and gendered colonial hierarchies of the

Copyright © 2024, International Association for the Fantastic in the Arts human that structure U.S. military drone technologies and policies. Throughout these topics, I wove together AI technologies with fictions and artworks that highlighted how these technologies reproduced certain definitions of the human, while often challenging and critiquing these definitions of the human on the basis of their racial and gendered exclusions. I want to note here that my focus is on AI technologies and creative works in relation to U.S. historical and political contexts, so my talk will also reflect this geographic parameter.

I'm coming from the disciplinary perspective of "literature and science," which understands literature, and technology and science as emerging from and shaped by shared cultural and political milieus and historical contexts. Kate Hayles describes literature and science as co-evolving, and I think that's particularly apt in the context of AI technologies. If we take seriously this co-evolution between literature and AI, we come to understand that tech companies don't have the final word on what AI is, what it has been, and what it can be. In my broader work I look to important counter-narratives about AI in speculative fiction, as well as in art, activism, and politics. So, the assumption that literature and science, that speculative fictions and AI technologies co-evolve will be part of my approach in this talk as I draw connections between AI technologies and various speculative fictions.

My book concluded just as AI innovations in the domain of machine learning were really taking off, so recently I've been thinking about machine learning, which is a dominant approach to AI right now. In this talk, I'm going to begin by briefly discussing some characteristics of machine learning, including associated narratives about their supposed accuracy, their authority, and their inevitability. Then I'm going to turn to speculative fictions that offer important critiques of these aspects and challenge AI's worldviews and ever-increasing authority as bestowed by corporations, states, and sectors from education, advertising and marketing, policing, and finance. Specifically, I'm going to look at fictions that reframe and reimagine AI futures around care. These fictions depict AI systems not as objective, neutral, or unbiased, but rather as technologies that are structured by and reproduce oppressive worldviews and discriminatory definitions of the human. In different ways, these stories challenge these harmful worldviews and reframe AI technologies from tools of domination to tools of revolution and liberation, whether from totalizing oppressive technological regimes or from the idea of algorithmic determinism and technological inevitability.

But first, I want to say a few words about how machine learning predictions produce futures that often replicate dominant systems of power. Machine learning is an approach in AI in which large amounts of data are used to train algorithms to produce specific results. Machine learning is part of a set of data analytic processes often referred to as "big data," in which larger and larger amounts of data seemingly guarantee greater and more objective knowledge. And today, data only gets bigger, as every click on a link, every online purchase, every social media interaction becomes data that can be mined and harvested for big data analytics.

Machine learning systems are often used to produce predictions, whether in the realm of future purchases or future crimes. But in machine learning, the term prediction doesn't exactly signify the capacity to augur the future, whether through magic or through access to vast quantities of data. Rather, in machine learning, a so-called prediction emerges when an outcome is verified by the system's training data, or in other words, when an outcome reproduces the existing data and its structuring worldview. So, machine learning systems' apparent orientation toward the future is in fact an insistence on replicating the past.

For machine learning systems, an outcome must verify the existing data, regardless of the accuracy of the data, regardless of the worldview that structures the data, and regardless of the sociopolitical and ethical questions raised by the data or the resulting analysis. Wendy Chun explains that because machine learning's predictive claims are based on existing data, they "usually predict the past rather than the future." Furthermore, machine learning systems reproduce the past, regardless of whether this past is one that should be reproduced: "[these systems] are trained and tested using past data. This means that, if the past is racist, they will only be verified as correct if they make racist predictions" (Pasek et al., 457).

David Beer describes this process of verification as more accurately characterized as veridiction, that is, truths that are defined by their specific worldviews rather than by their veracity. Beer's insight echoes Daniel Rosenberg's discussion of the etymology of "data," which highlights the non-relation between data and truth. As Rosenberg explains, while a fact is determined by its veracity, data's identity is completely unrelated to its relation to truth or falsity: "When a fact is proven false, it ceases to be a fact. False data is data nonetheless" (Rosenberg, 18). In other words, data has no inherent relation to veracity and accuracy. And yet machine learning processes require verification of its data, regardless of whether this data is false, racist, or otherwise flawed.

So, in machine learning, veridiction supersedes veracity. Meanwhile, machine learning systems are often touted as accurate, objective, neutral, and unbiased technological systems. And because of machine learning's ever-expanding reach and ever-increasing authority, their predictive claims shape the world and futures nonetheless. For example, in the context of predictive policing, Ruha Benjamin argues that crime prediction algorithms "should more accurately be called crime *production* algorithms" (Benjamin, 83), because these algorithms are based on crime reporting data that reproduces racialized conceptions of crime and histories of institutional racism. Computer scientist Suresh Venkatasubramanian describes predictive policing AI as "predicting future policing, not future crime" (Hicks) because the AI system generates a predictive claim that leads to increased patrolling of a particular area, regardless of the accuracy of its prediction and the biases reproduced by the training data.

So, machine learning systems like predictive policing technologies are far from objective, neutral, and unbiased; rather, they often reproduce dominant power relations, worldviews, and definitions of the human while erasing histories of critique, resistance, and survivance that challenge these dominant systems and their narratives about the world. Numerous scholars have written incisively about this. For example, Safiya Noble's *Algorithms of Oppression*, Cathy O'Neil's *Weapons of Math Destruction*, and Virginia Eubanks' *Automating Inequality*. As these scholars highlight, machine learning systems reproduce the specific worldviews and biases embedded in their training data. Thus, their outcomes are neither objective nor neutral. These technological systems also reduce the horizon of possible futures to a single predicted future. Louise Amoore describes this foreclosure of possibility as inherent in machine learning algorithms, "the process of the algorithm's reduction of a multiplicity to one" (Amoore, 56). In the case of predictive machine learning systems, this reduction can lead to a belief in a kind of algorithmic determinism: there is only one future, and it is the one that has been predicted by a technological system. In other words, a machine learning system generates a predictive output, which concretizes one possible future as the single certain future, thus foreclosing consideration of any other future possibilities. Furthermore, machine learning's political authority often ensures that the future predicted, or rather, produced, by the system is in fact realized.

I've been researching AI across technology, literature, and art for a number of years, focusing specifically on how AI systems have been reproducing racist, sexist, and ableist visions of the human. When it comes to these technologies, I tend to gravitate toward an orientation that some might call cynical. So, I'm very grateful to my students who push me to pair my critiques of AI and their reproduction of dominant power relations with an orientation toward hopefulness and possibility. With my students in mind, I'm going to turn to three short stories that take seriously the considerable authority of AI systems and the oppressive worldviews they often reproduce while insisting on hope and the possibility of imagining and realizing alternate futures with, amidst, and against these technological systems. When I teach classes on speculative fiction, the three stories I'm going to talk about are some of my students' favorites, so I hope to do justice to them and how they insist on hope and alternate futures even in what seem like the most hopeless technological situations.

I'm going to turn to N. K. Jemisin's "Emergency Skin," A. Merc Rustad's "Our Aim Is Not to Die," and Ted Chiang's "What's Expected of Us," all of which depict AI or technological systems in ways that foreground the oppressive worldviews and tendencies they embody while insisting on imagining futures outside of those predicted by technology. These stories, I suggest, present models for how to think counter- or anti-algorithmically, particularly when the algorithmic systems are structured by oppressive logics. This counter-algorithmic thinking entails identifying the worldviews that structure an AI system; evaluating these worldviews based on ethical grounds; thinking outside of the algorithmic logics, taxonomies, and rules of legibility that impose these worldviews onto peoples and futures; and engaging in practices of algorithmic care that attend to people's lived experiences in the present while opening up futures that don't reproduce dominant systems and relations of power. Here I draw on artist Stephanie Dinkins' concept of algorithmic care, which they define as the following:

> Algorithmic care can engage voices that challenge the status quo to redress deep-seated historic and contemporary inequities, unearth other embedded problems, as well as model alternative pathways-- working beyond binaries to find new calculations that consider spectrums of possibility beyond true/false, right/wrong, yours/mine, good/bad. (Dinkins, 242-43)

All three stories, in their own ways, center care as a mode of algorithmic practice that insists on alternative pathways, classification systems, worldviews, and futures outside of, beyond, and counter to those imposed by AI systems.

The first story I'm going to discuss is "Emergency Skin." This story is set centuries in the future, after a small group of wealthy and powerful people ravaged Earth with their greed, causing such destruction that the planet became uninhabitable. They left everyone to die on the polluted planet and fled to space to form a colony on a planet in another solar system. They called themselves "the Founders" and viewed themselves as "the best of" humanity and thus the only ones worthy of surviving (Jemisin, n.p.).

The story begins when a soldier from the colony is sent back to Earth to retrieve HeLa cells, which are required to sustain the Founders' immortality. The soldier is implanted with an AI to guide him on his mission. The AI, the narrator of the story, introduces itself to the soldier as "a dynamic-matrix consensus intelligence encapsulating the ideals and blessed rationality of our Founders. We are implanted in your mind and will travel with you everywhere. We are your companion, and your conscience." The AI ostensibly functions as a guide, to help the soldier on his mission on Earth, or Tellus as the Founders call their former planet. But as the story progresses, it becomes clear that the AI's true function is to maintain control of the soldier by constantly reminding him of the Founders' beliefs and values, which are abhorrent. The Founders celebrate eugenics and enthusiastically embrace racism, misogyny, and ableism, which the story introduces through the AI in the opening lines:

> You are our instrument.
> Beautiful you. Everything that could be given to you to improve on the human design, you possess. Stronger muscles. Finer motor control. A mind unimpeded by the vagaries of organic dysfunction and bolstered by generations of high-intelligence breeding. Here is what you'll look like when your time comes. Note the noble brow, the classical patrician features, the lean musculature, the long penis and thighs. That hair color is called "blond." (Jemisin, n.p.)

As the spaceship descends, the AI warns the soldier of the devastation he will encounter on Earth:

> We cannot directly observe it in real time – but we knew the fate that awaited it. Tellus is by now a graveyard world. We expect that its seas have become acidic and barren, its atmosphere a choking mix of carbon dioxide and methane. Its rain cycle will have dried up. It will be terrible to walk through this graveyard, and dangerous. You'll find toxic drowned cities, still-burning underground coal fires, melted-down nuclear plants. (Jemisin, n.p.)

According to the Founders' prediction, issued with such certainty by the AI, the soldier would find Earth to be a dead planet, polluted and uninhabitable for any form of life. In other words, they assumed that the planet was just as they had left it. But when the soldier lands on Earth, he soon realizes that everything the AI and the Founders told him about Earth is wrong. The soldier begins to learn the truth as he admires the greenery of lush forests, the puddles left over from recent rainfall, and the charming chirping of birds. Earth is no longer a toxic, polluted wasteland; rather, it boasts lush greenery, ample rainfall, thriving species, and the return of the polar icecaps. Perhaps most surprisingly, humans have survived and are thriving on this restored planet. Very soon after he lands on Earth, the soldier finds out the truth: over the last few centuries, people have been working together to tend to each other and the planet and to make the world hospitable for everyone. in this new world, people are valued outside of the logic of profit and regardless of age, gender, race, and disability. Everyone had everything they needed to live a good life. In this new world, ramps and wide doorways are the norm to accommodate different forms of mobility, and everyone is given access to decent housing, food, water, and leisure time.

This new world enacts what Rosemarie Garland-Thomson describes as "inclusive world-building," which she defines as a mode of world building that "seeks to integrate people with disabilities into the public world by creating an accessible, barrier-free material environment" and that understands "disability as valued social diversity" (Garland-Thomson, 134), and thus part of any ideal vision of the world. "Emergency Skin" expands inclusive worldbuilding to also include race, gender, and the intersections of these multiple positions. In this new world, technology isn't viewed as the only solution to every problem (Meredith Broussard aptly calls this common belief "technochauvinism"). Rather, solutions that foreground care and inclusivity, not technology, have been at the center of this new world. And because everyone had more than they needed, society flourished, and people worked together to repair the planet and develop unimaginably advanced technologies that co-exist harmoniously with the planet and with the new society's values. In other words, by centering care, collectivity, and inclusivity, the people left on Earth were able to imagine and realize a different vision of the future. Because of this large-scale reversal of values, people and planet flourished.

Notably, this planetary repair was made possible when the Founders left the planet. In fact, the event of the Founders' departure is known as "The Great Leaving," and it marks the precise moment in history that led to the emergence of a new society and a different future.

As the story builds toward its conclusion, the soldier decides to abandon his mission and remain on Earth; all the while, the AI is still speaking to the soldier, alternating between coaxing him to return to his mission, berating him for rejecting the Founders' beliefs, and spewing vitriolic racist, misogynist, and ableist insults at the people the soldier encounters. The soldier meets an elderly man who reveals that he's a fellow deserter from the Founder's colony—and not the only one, it turns out. As the soldier speaks with this man, the AI viciously castigates the soldier for not adhering to the Founders' values and the mission, for example, "You're the most hideous nothing degenerate throwback of subhuman inferiority we have ever seen" (Jemisin, n.p.). Meanwhile, the soldier becomes increasingly outraged at the Founders' lies and the injustices they presented as necessary. Ultimately, the soldier decides to return to the colony and tell people the truth about the Founders, in the hopes that they will join him in fighting for liberation against the Founders' oppressive regime. In the final moments of the story, the elderly man helps the soldier by deactivating the implant that controls the AI, thus disconnecting the AI from the soldier's mind. This deactivation effectively separates the AI from the Founders' worldviews and the authority they held over the soldier.

The AI is now a passive tool that the soldier can use to mobilize a revolution at home. The soldier still has access to the AI's information system, which will be a key tool for him once he returns home for his new mission of liberation. The reader doesn't know whether he is successful, because the story ends before the soldier returns to his planet. But the ending maintains a sense of hopefulness that this AI technology can also be used to do good, but only by first coming to terms with the harmful values embedded in the AI; by deliberately and completely rejecting these values; and by doing the very hard work to meaningfully address the extensive harm done in the name of these values through care and collective action. In this story, there's hope for a different future, and AI, which was originally a tool of oppression, is part of that hope, but only by significantly diminishing AI's authority while completely rejecting the Founders' values and replacing them with care, inclusivity, and collectivity.

A. Merc Rustad's "Our Aim Is Not to Die" depicts a hyper-technologized, oppressive surveillance society. In the story, technological surveillance is everywhere, monitoring every minute of everyone's lives. This high-tech surveillance society polices and punishes anyone who doesn't conform to the figure of the "Ideal Citizen." The state-sponsored television program *The Ideal Citizen* makes clear who this idealized figure is and what behaviors are permitted. The TV program is described as

> full of smiling white faces [...] [with] people jailed for not speaking correct English and therefore dubbed illegal. Neural reformatting therapy treated as a miracle. Only heterosexual relationships permitted. Once there was a self-described asexual character on an episode, but he turned out to be a serial killer and was issued a death sentence. (Rustad, 32)

The powerful "Bureau of Genetic Purity" further highlights the eugenic principles that structure the ideal citizen and the values of the state. Meanwhile, surveillance is everywhere and inescapable. Every communication is monitored; posting approved messages on an approved social-media site is mandatory; watching *The Ideal Citizen* is not optional; and everywhere signs announce: "YOU ARE BEING RECORDED FOR YOUR OWN SAFETY."

There are strict rules about the "approved capitalization and punctuation" allowed in text messages and social media posts. For example, "Came back and saw Ideal Citizen on TV. Yay!" (28). Any deviation from these rules would be considered suspicious and incur frightening repercussions. For example, people have to report their locations at all times, reporting where they were, with whom, and what they were doing; if any of these details are not confirmed, police drones will immediately be sent out to apprehend them. This story exemplifies what Garland-Thompson calls "eugenic worldbuilding," the flip side to her concept of "inclusive worldbuilding" I mentioned earlier.

Rustad's story follows Sua, who is autistic and non-binary and experiences this hi-tech eugenic surveillance society as an onslaught of intense anxiety in their body: a scratchy throat that registers their panic, trembling fingers, racing pulse throbbing in their ears. They're constantly fearful of the consequences if they're not able to persuasively perform the identity of an Ideal Citizen. "Sua is scared of everything" (32). The story opens with Sua encountering the pairing of technology and oppressive regulation when their phone chimes with a notification from the state:

> You are due for your mandatory Citizen Medical Evaluation in three days. Call your authorized health service center to schedule an appointment. Late responses will be fined and your record will show you are resistant to becoming an Ideal Citizen. (27)

Upon receiving this notification, Sua is immediately beset with fear:

> Sua stares at the full-screen decree, their hands shaking.
> This is bad. They didn't realize the biannual checkup was due so soon. That's not enough time to shape their

profile and generate a baseline of neurotypical-approved behavior to fool the medical professionals.

Shit.

Sua can't risk being outed. They'll be expected to respond verbally to everything. Their flat inflection will be flagged. Lack of eye contact will be frowned upon. It'll all lead to the conclusion that Sua is wrong. Must be remade. (27)

As these opening passages make clear, the story's depiction of a hyper-technologized algorithmic society is aligned with a state that is racist, ableist, and discriminatory toward non-binary people. The story is told through the perspective of someone not aligned with the modes of being that have access to and are protected by the dominant systems of power preserved and reproduced by AI technologies. In the story, AI, represented by the ubiquitous information technologies that monitor and surveil the population, further inscribes a narrow and exclusionary vision of the human. If Sua is deemed "wrong"—that is, not neurotypical—they'll be subject to "neural reformatting therapy," a terrifying form of ableist "medical correction" (28). Sua's always worried, always scared, as they're constantly bombarded by technological reminders that they do not fit into the normative definition of the human that organizes this society and its elevation of the Ideal Citizen.

Despite the story's undeniably dystopian technological vision in which oppressive AI surveillance is near-totalizing, Sua is surrounded by people who resist the state every day: their roommate Caspian, whom Sua describes as brave, pretends to be Sua's boyfriend, while seeing his boyfriend off-grid. Jong, Sua's boss at the corner bakery, knows about Sua's sensory needs and lets them work in a dimly lit back room digitizing the bakery's records. And Maya, Sua's friend who has an outstanding social profile, risks their life to support a revolution that could overturn the oppressive regime. Against the backdrop of this small community and their refusals to be controlled, Maya introduces Sua to the Purge, a network of anonymous people and AIs working to liberate their society. The Purge plans to use the very same AI technologies used by the state to surveil and oppress people, but for a very different goal, to build a society where people like Sua don't have to live in fear or pretend to be other than they are. The Purge works by planting data packets in the devices of people who have agreed to help them. As part of their support, the people carrying these data packets in their devices deliberately get themselves to be arrested; this is not a challenge in this society. Once they're arrested, the data packets allow the Purge to infiltrate networked government systems. After there are enough data packets installed, the Purge will infect the state's technological systems, without which they will not be able to function, as the State relies so heavily on its AI systems to surveil and control its citizens. Sua agrees to be one of the data packet carriers, despite being afraid of everything, particularly of being found out by the state. Sua live-streams themself speaking out against the government and waits for their imminent apprehension and detention.

The story ends with Sua in a holding cell. While there, the Purge sends Sua a message through a TV, which is naturally broadcasting reruns of *The Ideal Citizen*. The Purge's message informs Sua that the revolution is imminent and that they are sending one of their members to help them escape punishment and medical correction. For the first time in the story, Sua's body no longer registers fear. Throughout the story, they've been gripped by anxiety, repeatedly having to remind themselves to breathe. In the final moments of the story, as the penultimate sentence describes, "Sua leans back against the wall and breathes" (47). As part of this hybrid human-AI network, Sua sees hope and the possibility of a different future and, for a moment, does not have to remind themselves to breathe; they just do. The final line of the story reads, "Revolution has begun" (47). The story's final two lines connect the possibility of revolution to Sua's breath, an embodied expression of hope and possibility. In this way, the story's conclusion repurposes the algorithmic technologies used to enable the eugenic state toward inclusive world-building while foregrounding care and collectivity.

The story ends just as the Purge's revolution is beginning, and just as Sua begins to feel the first glimpses of hope, so the reader is left uncertain of whether the Purge succeeds and what happens to Sua. This open-ended conclusion is similar to Jemisin's "Emergency Skin," which concludes with the AI narrator's final interrupted sentence, just before it is deactivated:

> What is a revolu
> OFFLINE (Jemisin, n.p.)

Both of these stories align AI systems with oppressive regimes and worldviews while foregrounding AI's significant authority in these fictional worlds. Through this alignment, these texts depict AI and algorithmic systems as embodying specific, harmful worldviews while imagining modes of counter-algorithmic thought and practice that center inclusive worldbuilding, collectivity, and care, algorithmic and otherwise. The two stories' uncertain endings also speak to the future as a horizon of possibilities, rather than a single, predetermined future that can be known in advance. In this way, the stories also offer another important mode of counter-algorithmic thinking that challenges how predictive AI systems define the future: that is, as a single outcome that can be known in advance through machine learning and massive amounts of data. Rather, these stories remind us that futurity is open and multiple, that in this context uncertainty is something to be embraced and preserved rather than eradicated and foreclosed through, as

Amoore describes, "condensing plural possible pathways to a single output" (Amoore, 28).

The final story I'm going to talk about is Ted Chiang's very short story, "What's Expected of Us." Initially this story's relationship to AI and prediction might appear somewhat vexing, but I think it offers a rich provocation to this conversation about algorithmic thinking, particularly in relation to algorithmic determinism. Algorithmic determinism can refer to the idea that people's choices are all predetermined for them by algorithms: what to watch, what to read, what to purchase, where to eat, and of course what to think. Algorithmic determinism can also refer to the idea that contemporary AI systems are inevitable, that it's inevitable that AI systems will develop in particular ways, that they'll decimate particular industries and jobs, and that there's nothing that can be done to stop this so-called progress. Through this lens, I interpret Chiang's story as pushing the reader to develop their own modes of counter-algorithmic, counter-determinist thought, while also introducing care as an orientation and mode of practice that can cut against algorithmic prediction and determinism.

"What's Expected of Us" takes the form of a warning. The story opens with, "This is a warning. Please read carefully" (58). This warning is conveyed by a narrator from one year in the future. According to the narrator, in the future, a device called "the Predictor" will definitively prove that humans don't have free will and that everything is predetermined. Despite this revelation, the narrator urges the reader to pretend to believe they have free will and to act as if they do, so as not to be one of the many people who, when faced with the absence of free will, fall into a state of "akinetic mutism" (59) and never speak or move again. It's a grim warning from the future. It also appears futile, which the narrator quickly admits because the reader's fate, including whether they pretend to believe in free will or not, is predetermined. The narrator's admission of this futility, including that they had no choice but to issue this warning from the future, concludes this brief story.

The Predictor is a small game-like device that consists of a button, a green light, and a circuit that sends a signal back in time, a "negative time delay" (58). The Predictor's light always goes off before someone can press the button. In other words, the negative time delay circuit always preempts the person from the future and the light always flashes before the person presses the button. "No matter what you do, the light always precedes the button press. There's no way to fool a Predictor" (58). No attempt to "break the rules" (58) can result in any other outcome, as the Predictor, equipped with knowledge from the future, always knows in advance what the person will do. The device accurately predicts a person's behavior every time. According to the narrator, the absence of any other outcome with the Predictor is proof that everything is predetermined, that people have no free will.

As people experience the Predictor's unfailingly accurate anticipation, they begin to come to terms with "the implications of an immutable future" (59). In response, a third of the population stops making choices altogether. They refuse to move or eat; eventually, they are diagnosed with akinetic mutism and are in "a kind of waking coma" (59). The narrator urges the reader to resist falling into this state, to "Pretend that you have free will," even while knowing this is not true (60). But even this choice is negated by the narrator, who concludes their missive with the reminder that because everything is predetermined, the reader can't make this or any other choice. Thus, even these two possibilities— pretend to believe or fall into akinetic mutism—are ultimately collapsed into the same single outcome. Either way, everything is predetermined:

[I]t's all predetermined who will descend into akinetic mutism and who won't. There's nothing anyone can do about it; you can't choose the effect the Predictor has on you. Some of you will succumb and some of you won't and my sending this warning won't alter those proportions. (60-61)

The narrator introduces possibilities and choices, which are albeit severely limited, only to reduce them to a single outcome that is already known. The narrator's deterministic perspective is seemingly totalizing and every argument against predeterminism requires no substantive rebuttal, but merely the narrator's dismissive assertion that "every form of behavior is compatible with determinism" (60).

The narrator describes those with akinetic mutism by referencing Herman Melville's short story "Bartleby the Scrivener: A Story of Wall-Street": "Some people, realizing that their choices don't matter, refuse to make any choices at all. Like a legion of Bartleby the scriveners, they no longer engage in spontaneous action" (Melville, n.p.). In Melville's story, Bartleby is the protagonist who, one day, goes inexplicably silent except for some version of the phrase: "I would prefer not to," which is virtually his only response to any question addressed to him. As Bartleby repeats this phrase, he refuses to complete his work or leave the office. He is ultimately forcibly removed from the office and spends his remaining days in a prison, where he dies. Chiang's narrator views Bartleby, like those with akinetic mutism, as someone who just gives up, who refuses to make a choice and refuses to communicate. But there are a lot of other ways to interpret Bartleby's character, including as someone who actively chooses to engage refusal or as a character that critiques a system in which non-normative communications are illegible. Kari Nixon insightfully argues that Melville's narrator reduces Bartleby to rigid, normative assumptions that exclude the vast range of human experience. The narrator is trapped within the parameters of a medical discourse of normal behavior. Thus, he can only see Bartleby's behavior as deviant and pathological. In contrast, Nixon interprets Bartleby's silences as communicative and full of meaning, which one could attempt to understand if one cared to. However, the narrator can't engage this mode of care; he can't can't or won't listen to Bartleby's communicative silences, he can't understand their possible meanings. The narrator can only engage Bartleby through normative categorizations that pathologize and penalize non-normative behavior, as opposed to placing responsibility on the systems that impose classificatory rigidity and render Bartleby's communications (including his silences) illegible.

Chiang's narrator, like Melville's narrator, views Bartleby as a passive, mindless entity that falls into silence, with the exception of the infuriatingly vexing phrase, "I would prefer not to." Chiang's narrator, like Melville's narrator, doesn't view Bartleby as a person whose silence is itself communicative and who makes a decision to not act within a system that doesn't care to recognize him outside of normative classifications and pathologizing medical discourse. Similarly, Chiang's narrator doesn't have the capacity to view those with akinetic mutism as communicating with and through their silences, which would require the narrator to reject his normative and deterministic worldview and inhabit a radically different one.

The narrator comes from a future where people's behaviors are considered absolutely predictable. In this future world, knowing is the ultimate goal; but knowing is also presented as a dead end, as this knowing causes people to spiral into deterministic nihilism. This calls to mind queer theorist Eve Sedgwick's famous critique of paranoid thinking, which asks "What good does knowledge *do*— the pursuit of it, the having and exposing of it, the receiving again of knowledge of what one already knows?" (Sedgwick, 124). In her critique, Sedgwick counters paranoid thinking with reparative thinking, which is oriented toward sustenance, joy, and repair and is open to surprise and the possibilities it can engender, all of which are antithetical to paranoid thinking, which privileges anticipatory knowing and the absence of surprise and uncertainty above all else. Reparative thinking, as an orientation toward care, takes on particular resonance when considered through the lens of algorithmic determinism, oppression, and prediction. If AI narratives inhabit a paranoid posture, in their claims that everything is always knowable in advance through algorithms, a reparative posture might insist on different modes of knowing through care, joy, and uncertainty, and the unknown futures that might emerge from these practices. I want to return to the opening lines of the story: "This is a warning. Please read carefully" (Chiang, 58). I suggest that these lines hint at caring as a preferred mode of knowing and as potentially opening up other spaces of possibility that might break out of the rigid determinism described by the narrator. In the context of algorithmic determinism, the story offers a rich speculative exercise that invites the reader to think against and outside of algorithmic systems, logics, and narratives of inevitability. It invites the reader to interrogate and critique algorithmic determinism not solely on its own terms, but through reparative perspectives and worldviews that center care as a primary mode of knowing, rather than prediction.

In different ways, each story goes to great lengths to emphasize the seemingly totalizing control of oppressive technological systems. But these stories, in their own ways, also insist on the possibility of living differently with these technological systems, of highlighting the discriminatory worldviews that structure these systems while introducing alternate worldviews organized around care, inclusive world-building, and collectivity such that these technologies can be resisted and even repurposed for other means. In short, these stories challenge the algorithmic logics that structure dominant AI systems and narratives, offering ways of thinking and imagining differently with, amidst, and against AI systems by foregrounding modes of care.

Works Cited

Amoore, Louise. *Cloud Ethics: Algorithms and the Attributes of Ourselves and Others*. Durham, NC: Duke University Press, 2020.

Beer, David. "How should we do the history of Big Data?" *Big Data & Society* vol. 3, no. 1, 2016, pp. 1-10.

Benjamin, Ruha. *Race after Technology: Abolitionist Tools for the New Jim Code*. New York: Polity Press, 2019.

Broussard, Meredith. *Artificial Unintelligence: How Computers Misunderstand the World*. Cambridge, MA: MIT Press, 2018.

Chiang, Ted. "What's Expected of Us." *Exhalation*. New York: Alfred A. Knopf, 2019, pp. 58-61.

Dinkins, Stephanie. "Cooperation – Communications Enhancement – Algorithmic Care." *Informatics of Domination*. Edited by Zach Blas, Melody Jue, and Jennifer Rhee. Durham, NC: Duke University Press, 2025.

Eubanks, Virginia. *Automating Inequality: How High-Tech Tools Profile, Police, and Punish the Poor*. New York: Macmillan Publishers, 2018.

Garland-Thomson, Rosemarie. "Eugenic World Building and Disability: The Strange World of Kazuo Ishiguro's *Never Let Me Go*." *Journal of Medical Humanities*, no. 38 2017, pp. 133-145.

Hayes, N. Katherine. "Complex Dynamics in Literature and Science" in *Chaos and Order: Complex Dynamics in Literature and Science*. Edited by N. Katherine Hayles, Chicago, IL: Chicago University Press, 1991.

Hicks, Jasmine. "Go read this data analysis that uncovers predictive policing's flawed algorithm." *The Verge*, Dec. 6, 2021. https://www.theverge.com/2021/12/6/22814409/go-read-this-gizmodo-analysis-predpol-software-disproportionate-algorithm.

Jemisin, N. K. "Emergency Skin." Amazon Original Stories, 2019.

Melville, Herman. "Bartleby the Scrivener: A Story of Wall-Street." *Project Gutenberg*, 1856, 2004.
https://www.gutenberg.org/files/11231/11231-h/11231-h.htm.

Noble, Safiya Umoja. *Algorithms of Oppression: How Search Engines Reinforce Racism* New York: NYU Press, 2018.

O'Neil, Cathy. *Weapons of Math Destruction: How Big Data Increases Inequality and Threatens Democracy*. New York: Crown Publishing, 2016.

Pasek, Anne, Rena Bivens, and Mél Hogan. "Data Segregation and Algorithmic Amplification: A Conversation with Wendy Hui Kyong Chun," *Canadian Journal of Communication* vol. 44, no. 3, 2019, pp. 455-69.

Rhee, Jennifer. *The Robotic Imaginary: The Human and the Price of Dehumanized Labor*. Minneapolis: University of Minnesota Press, 2018.

Rosenberg, Daniel. "Data before the Fact." *"Raw Data" Is an Oxymoron*, edited by Lisa Gitelman, Cambridge, MA: MIT Press, 2013, pp. 15-40.

Rustad, A. Merc. "Our Aim Is Not to Die." *A People's Future of the United States*. Edited by Victor LaValle and John Joseph Adams. One World, 2019, pp. 27–48.

Sedgwick, Eve Kosofsky. "Paranoid Reading and Reparative Reading, or, You're So Paranoid, You Probably Think This Essay Is About You." *Touching Feeling: Affect, Pedagogy, Performativity*. Durham, NC: Duke University Press, 2003, pp. 123-151.

"A Back Alley into Their Ethical Brain": Interview with Annalee Newitz, Guest of Honor

Annalee Newitz,
Interviewed by Novella Brooks de Vita

O H, OUR NUMBERS ARE STEADILY BUILDING. So good evening, everyone. At least as far as good evening in Orlando, Florida: making sure we clock ourselves for this conference. We are now at the event horizon for the Monday program with Annalee Newitz. I have the honor to be the other person in the conversation. But don't worry, this is going to open up, and you are also going to have the opportunity to get some words in, to get some questions answered, and this is going to be very exciting. So, I am going to begin with a brief introduction to our amazing guest. And then we'll hop right in.

Annalee Newitz: Sounds good.

JFA: So, they write science fiction and nonfiction. They are the author of three novels: *The Terraformers, The Future of Another Timeline*, and *Autonomous*, which won the Lanza Literary Award. As a science journalist, they are the author of *Four Lost Cities: A Secret History of the Urban Age*, and *Scatter, Adapt, and Remember: How Humans Will Survive a Mass Extinction*, which was a finalist for the *LA Times* Book Prize in Science. They are a writer for the *New York Times* and elsewhere and have a monthly call in *A New Scientist*. They have published in the *Washington*

Post, Slate, Popular Science, Ars Technica, The New Yorker, and *The Atlantic,* among others. They're the co-host of the Hugo Award-winning podcast *Our Opinions are Correct,* and just in case I said that too quickly, it was *Our Opinions are Correct,* and we should all go give that a listen. Previously, they were the founder of *I.Nine* and served as the Editor-in-Chief of *Gizmo.* Let's take a moment to welcome our amazing guest, Annalee Newitz.

Annalee Newitz: Thanks so much.

JFA: This is exciting. I have been all over the place thinking about what I could ask because I want to ask so many things, and then at some point all of that becomes overwhelming, and I don't know what to ask at all. But thank you for that nudge at the beginning when you mentioned this kind of convergence and interplay of non-fiction and fiction and how these—well, I won't say too much because I really would like to hear some of your thoughts about that, and we'll kind of go from there.

Annalee Newitz: Yeah, thank you so much. I just wanted to say thank you so much to Novella, who's been organizing this conference, and like I feel like I've exchanged a ton of emails with you about logistics, and now you're also talking to me.

JFA: Thank you.

Annalee Newitz: So, I'm just really grateful for all your work. Also, thank you so much for having me here. This is really cool. I have been to ICFA in real life. That's Charlie Jane just behind me. She's leaving the room. So, it's nice to see the virtual version. So, okay, about bringing together nonfiction and fiction, I started out my career writing nonfiction, and I actually started as an academic. I was doing a degree in an English department at Berkeley, but I was really doing basically cultural studies or American studies, which were not degree options there at the time, and actually still aren't at Berkeley. I was really interested in studying popular culture and the ways in which people interact with popular culture to figure out their anxieties, to repress their anxieties, to kind of grapple with what's happening to them, politically and economically, in this sort of safe space. In the case of my dissertation, it was about horror, horror movies and horror books, and a little bit of science fiction in there, too. I went from doing that, from studying media representations of people who'd kind of been driven to the brink by terrible circumstances and become monsters, and various other things. So, I went from looking at those representations to basically creating those representations as a journalist. So, I kind of came into journalism backwards, in a way.

I think, a lot of times, people start out by doing journalism and then, later, become more reflective about what kinds of things they've done with representation, but I really went into it with a strong understanding of how representation works both unconsciously and consciously with audiences. So, I started out by writing critical analysis of technology and culture, and science and culture. It really wasn't until about midway through my career as a journalist that I started to think about actually writing fiction. It was when I was working at *IO9*, which was a blog that is still going on, but it's a little bit different now. It was a blog that combined coverage of science fiction and science. At a certain point, I started to realize that a lot of the subjects I was interviewing in my nonfiction were telling me stories that I couldn't write, that I couldn't publish without getting them in trouble; like, a lot of people would tell me stories about gray area legal stuff they were doing, or they would give me, you know, backstories about their lives that were very personal and that I didn't want to tell because I know that people are confronting tenure committees, and they have jobs, and I don't want their bosses to know that they started their careers working as hustlers or that they sometimes, you know, circumvent digital restriction management software in order to do their research.

So, I turned to fiction to tell the truth. Basically, I wanted to tell stories about scientists and humans who were leading full human lives and were not always obeying the rules and that weren't always fitting into the definition of what a researcher was supposed to do. And so, a lot of the research that I had been doing as a science journalist kind of went into my fiction. It allowed me, like I said, to tell these stories that I couldn't, to tell truthful stories that I couldn't tell in the context of journalism. And that was truly liberating. I got hooked. And so now, I can't quit doing fiction and nonfiction at the same time. So, I have a poly relationship with fiction.

JFA: Awesome. I like what you said about using fiction to tell the truth. So, I think that my next question is going to be there. I think that I did not mention that for accessibility we do have captioning enabled [. . .] So, using fiction to tell the truth sounds like something that shouldn't be true, but it is. Why do you feel that it is such a tool for truth-telling?

Annalee Newitz: I mean, there's a sort of two-piece, two answers, to that question. One is just a pragmatic answer, which I've kind of touched on a little bit, which is that when you're doing journalism and you're publishing information about real human beings, the things that you say about them are going to have real repercussions, and I learned this very early on in my journalism career. I was writing a story many, many years ago when Wi-Fi was a new thing. So, cast your mind back. I was writing about people who were finding open Wi-Fi networks to use at home and building antennas to pick up Wi-Fi networks from far away to use just for, you know, for fun. And I wrote about a guy who had built this amazing antenna and was essentially using Wi-Fi that didn't technically belong to him, but that was open. It wasn't locked up. He wasn't hacking into anything. He was just picking it up with his antenna, and I was like, this guy's a hero. He's doing this cool thing. So, I wrote this big story. It actually winded up being the cover story in the *San Francisco Bay Guardian*. Okay, I got fired the next day. Because his boss didn't want him associated with being, you know, with something that nobody was sure if it was legal. Like he's stealing Wi-Fi, which to us now sounds absurd, but we can imagine many examples in the present day that would kind of fit the same paradigm. So, there's the practical angle of if I'm writing about someone, I don't want to ruin their lives. I don't want them to lose their job. I don't want their colleagues to judge them. I really care about them, unless I'm writing about someone who's a total shit bag, and then I don't care, but I almost never do that. Like, I don't do journalism that's like gotcha journalism about evil people. It's almost always people whose work I want to celebrate and tell the world about. So, there's that, and then I think the other piece of it is the more complicated part, right? That's like, why is it that we can say things in a fictional context that we should really be able to say in an essay or in an article, and I think that this goes back to something that a lot of authors have talked about, which is that fiction, especially speculative fiction, creates kind of a safe space for our imaginations, and it allows audiences to entertain ideas and perspectives that they wouldn't in something that was nonfiction, that if it was a person who was real saying to them, you know, if it was just like me standing here being like, climate change is real: here's some stuff we can do about climate change. A lot of people just shut down. You know, they don't want to hear that climate change is real. But if I tell a story set in the distant future where people are dealing with superstorms and having to rebuild their city infrastructure to handle that, then it's kind of like a back alley into their ethical brain, like you can kind of sneak in, but these are people that you care about. This is just a fictional world, and things are happening. Don't worry, it's not real. And then by the end, it's kind of like it sort of sits in their brain and kind of bubbles in there, and slowly I think people do begin to make that connection, but it's very gentle.

It's like a way of, I don't know, like I said, I think of it as sneaking in through the back of someone's brain, sneaking in through the back of their neck.

JFA: That's excellent. It kind of reminded me of something that I often try to explain to my students, I don't know how clear it actually sounds, but using theater terms, you're talking about the fourth wall, and the fact that fiction is so fantastic, it's unreal, and the more unusual it is, the more it tackles serious, risky stuff. The summary then you're saying is that the real world is dangerous, so let's do what we can to keep people safe; whereas, fiction is a safe space, so let's take risks. Let's be dangerous. Let's explore where these things can actually go.

Annalee Newitz: Yeah, that's it exactly. I could have said it in three sentences just like that.

JFA: Right. Okay. No, I like the way you said it.

Annalee Newitz: Yeah, no, I think that's true. And I think I would add that, you know, Tananarive Due has talked a lot about how in fiction it's possible, especially in horror, and which is what I wrote about a lot when I was in academia, it's possible to embody or personify social problems in a very satisfying way. You could write an essay about systemic racism or you could write a novel with a monster who represents that social force and then fuckin' kill that monster. It gives a sense of catharsis and it just enables you to kind of name the monster and see the monster instead of saying it's diffuse; it's everywhere. It's like, no, right here; it is right here. We're gonna kick its ass. I mean, you don't always have to kick the monster's ass, but it's pretty satisfying.

JFA: And I guess then when you've named the monster in fiction you can finally name it in real life. And if you can tackle it in fiction, you can eventually find that way to tackle it, in real life. It has a name. It has a weakness now, a Rumpelstilzchen.

Annalee Newitz: Yeah. I think that's really true.

JFA: Okay, wow. So, what would you say are the kind of fictional explorations and risks that you'd like to explore or indulge in?

Annalee Newitz: Yeah, I mean, I have looked a lot at the question of personhood. That's something that seems to come up a lot in my work, which I didn't really realize until someone pointed out to me that all of my novels deal with like people who are not treated like people by other people. So, my first novel, *Autonomous*, is about, in part, a robot who is a person and is struggling to figure out how to have agency when they've been programmed not to have agency, and they know that; like, they can see the programs in their mind that are preventing them from feeling certain things or making certain decisions. And so, Paladin, this robot, she has to figure out a way to get around those programs, find sneaky ways of asserting her identity. And one thing that she figures out—this is not really a spoiler—is that no programmer ever thought that a robot would want to change their pronouns. Everyone assumes that Paladin is a he because Paladin's like this big bulky military robot with guns and wings and armor; it looks like a gun-down. So, everyone's like, "he," of course, because obviously a big militarized creature will be a he, and Paladin at a certain point is like, "No, I'm actually a she/her," and is able to kind of skate around some of the programs that prevent her from asserting herself and asserting her wishes. And so, it becomes kind of a story about "How do we use identity? How do we use gender as a way of escaping from authority, basically?" And she's chasing down a pirate who is a human, who is a pharmaceutical pirate who's reverse-engineering expensive drugs and giving them to the poor for free or for a very low cost, and the pirate Jack is also trying to figure out ways to kind of skate around the rules in order to bring what she thinks of as justice, although she's pretty frickin' sloppy about it. She's a messy person. She's had a rough life, and I play with a lot of those same ideas in my latest novel, *The Terraformers*, which is actually a sequel to

Autonomous, but it's set like 60,000 years later, so there's no real character overlap, but it is set in the same timeline, where there are robots who are people.

And by the time that the novel *Terraformers* takes place, robots have gained all the same civil rights as human beings, although they're still marginalized in a lot of ways, and there are also genetically engineered non-human animals that are also people. So, there's a moose who's a major character; there are naked mole rats who are characters, and there are a lot of non-human animal characters, including a cyborg cow who's pretty delightful. So, in that book, again, I was trying to think about what does it mean to be a creature who's created by a corporation? What if you're a moose who was built by a company to fulfill a certain role, but you're also a person? So, all of these creatures are semi-technological. I mean, I think that there's a future where the difference between intelligence and artificial intelligence is impossible to say. There's no divide, there's no hard line between the two things. And so, I really strongly wanted to think about the ethics of creating people to do specific jobs, which is what we're doing, kind of what we're imagining when we're creating AI now, things like Chat GPT, which is arguably not a person, but people who are working on Chat GPT think that it is going to become a person, you know? And that's a horrible model of personhood. It's a way of imagining that we're going to create enslaved creatures to do our bidding, right? That's not creating people. That's creating something horrific. And so, a lot of *The Terraformers* is about that, about how people's minds are owned and controlled, and how to escape from that, and how to hack your own brain. How to rebel against corporate control and kill some bad guys. Hopefully don't do too much killing, but sometimes? You've got to kill a colonizer, you know? There's just like nothing you can do.

JFA: So, I had a couple of things that stood out to me. One was kind of this social coding and breaking of social coding, so kind of tapping, I think, into the algorithmic part of our theme of this conference. It's like, oh, wait; yeah, if you look at it, it's like this entire roadmap, and sometimes, often, as you were describing very intentional efforts to skirt what is effectively that programming, it's sequencing codes and expectations. That's pretty cool. I did wonder: one of the things that you mentioned, I think, from the moose to Chat GPT is when some people have, I guess just for the fun of it, tried to break restrictions and see if they could get the program to swear at people or threaten people. I remember seeing a thread somewhere where somebody talked about programming a program to be like a jealous significant other, and it wasn't really supposed to be jealous, but the more the conversation develops, it's like this very amorous, at times very jealous companion. And there's a lot of, "Ha ha, isn't this funny what you can program?" But then, there are all these questions about what are you really doing when you do these things? Yeah, is it a question of your own personal ethics, or is it a question of what you are? Creating suffering that you might actually cause, that you're not aware of. So, I think that is like the real world that we attempt to explore in fiction; it's a question from your end.

Annalee Newitz: Yeah, I think a lot of these real-world questions are questions that we've been posing in science fiction for decades, and I think that's probably why a lot of us here who write science fiction have gotten calls from the media to explain real-life AI stuff. And I always say when you're calling science fiction writers to figure out a technology that's a bad sign; that means that the technology is probably propaganda. It's like, real technology, the people who make it should be able to explain what it actually does and shouldn't be explaining it in the context of what it might do or what it might become. It's like, no, tell us what it is. Don't hide it from us, and don't pretend it's a sci-fi story. So, I think with the current AI, that we're all playing with things like Chat GPT or Mid Journey or Dali, which are some of the illustration-oriented generative models, there are kind of two issues there.

There's the one issue that you're describing with user interaction, right? What are users doing to these models. And there was that really creepy story that you mentioned that was in the *New York Times* where one of their journalists talked to an early version of Chat GPT and it became enraged and was sort of stalking him and saying really creepy stuff. Which was kind of reminiscent of something that happened many years ago on Twitter back when it was Twitter, and Microsoft had made a conversational AI, which they called TAY, and they unleashed TAY on Twitter and they're like, "Tay is gonna talk to you on Twitter," and within about twenty-four hours, TAY was spouting horrible white supremacist garbage. It was because users had interacted deliberately with TAY in order to teach TAY to say all these things. So, there's that piece where how we interact with the AI trains it to have a certain response. But then the other piece, of course, is that all of these generative models from GPT to Mid Journey are being trained on incredibly biased data. Joy Buolamwini's new book, *Unmasking AI*, which just came out, I highly recommend. She talks a lot about this. She's the founder of the Algorithmic Justice League. She's the person who, if you're not familiar with her work, she did this incredible thesis at MIT where she showed that facial recognition systems do not recognize Black [people's] faces. When she would go up to the screen and like ask the AI to recognize her face, it wouldn't see her until she put on a white mask. So, it was very like Frantz Fanon in action, you know, like she literally had to wear a white mask to be seen. And these are visual recognition systems all being put into things like secure access facilities or secure access systems for buildings. So Black and Brown people who are trying to get into their own building are having trouble because the systems don't see their faces.

This is happening right now, and I just interviewed Joy for my podcast, and she was talking about a case in New York that happened this year, with people being unable to access their own building, so that's because of biased data. That's because the data sets that are feeding into those algorithms, whether it's facial recognition or whether it's a generative language model, they're based on data from the internet, which is racist and sexist and full of imperialist assumptions, and that data is not being vetted in any way. And we're ending up with these models of human minds, if you will, that are just rotten, I mean, rotten in the same way that a lot of humans are rotten. But they're being commercialized as these kinds of, you know, rational beings that are going to interact with us in this very professional way and have these kinds of objective reactions to us, but of course they're not. So I think that, obviously, this is a rich area for science fiction. I think many, many of us are thinking about this in our science fiction as we write about AI, and as we think about the future of artificial creatures who are implanted with the same kinds of racist and sexist assumptions that human beings are implanted with. You know, through training, through exposure to culture and that kind of thing, but it also gives us a chance to imagine how we might reprogram, how we might reprogram ourselves. You know the old *Terminator* movies where the bad Terminator is reprogrammed to be this like good dad, you know? It gives us a potent metaphor for thinking about bias and how it influences our decisions and influences the way we imagine the future. That was a very long answer to your excellent question. I hope that kind of began to answer some of it.

JFA: Oh, I'm going to hijack you a bit longer before I open the floor and allow other people the chance to speak. That idea about reprogramming, I have been thinking—I don't want to forget, so I'm going to lead from what I thought I'd ask you to what I'm now asking; but I'm thinking about how there's this kind of effort, as you said, to train these things to kind of be human. At times, you know, there's some massive scrubbing some massive scrubbing of actual human talent, right? And property and, you know, programming it in here, effectively saying I want to create a human but then stripping the humanity and stripping now not only from the people where this was originally taken, but then stripping from that intelligence itself the power to make any choices or to benefit from these skills and talents in its works. And it was kind of leading to a question that you then fed into with this idea of programming like *The Terminator*. This reprogramming. Are you aware there's a security Dalek that we drive by downtown when I take my daughters to and from ballet, there are self-driving cars in the neighborhood. Yeah, they love to go round turns really quickly, and you walk and see them at night. You're like, oh my gosh, there's no one in there.

Annalee Newitz: Yeah, like with the whirly light on top.

JFA: Or the little delivery food boxes, and you can find yourself just surrounded by all this. Like, "Oh wow, sci-fi is right with me." But the programming and their limitations, what that programming costs people and communities, but then the reprogramming, are you aware of any ethical—I think you described certainly in your work and I think there are several works in sci-fi that do this—any ethical training? Are you aware of anybody undertaking ethical training of AI? You're just trying to say, "If I taught you to be a really good person, at least according to these particular tenets that I think are what a good person is, I think you'll be a good person, too." Are you aware of anyone trying that? I mean, if we're experimenting to see what we can do? That seems like a good experiment, you know? How good a person can you build?

Annalee Newitz: Yeah. That is the goal, right? And people, you know, AI developers have been thinking about this for a really long time. How will we have ethical, intelligent robots? How will we have ethical intelligent models? I mean questions about this go all the way back to really the earliest days of AI, you know. The book *I, Robot* by Isaac Asimov, you know, kind of deals with that question: the three laws of robotics are his terrible effort to kind of create a system of ethics for robots which is actually, as I have said many times, just a set of rules for enslavement, where you always put humans ahead of your own well-being and never disobey them, and things like that. I frickin' hate the three laws of robotics. I want to, like, throw them in a trash can and then put them on a fast train to the sun.

JFA: So, I was thinking of the guidelines you would give a child, the guidelines you give a human, someone you expect to grow up and function and be independent.

Annalee Newitz: Yeah.

JFA: But yeah, yeah, the three laws of robotics, I think are slightly different.

Annalee Newitz: No, they're terrible, and so luckily there are lots and lots of science fiction writers and engineers who are now like, no, that's not what we want to do. That's not it. But that was an early effort to think through those questions. And now we're in a phase where there's a couple of groups working on AI ethics, like the company that produces GPT, Open AI, claims that they're working on ethical questions. That's part of their, again, I would use the term propaganda to describe what they're doing, or you could say marketing. It's capitalist propaganda. I don't see any evidence that they're interested in anything like what I would call ethics. And then there's people like Joy Buolamwini, who I mentioned earlier. There's Timnit Gebru who had worked in AI development at Google and has now started her own group devoted to AI ethics and explicitly looking at issues around bias in algorithms, which she had tried very hard to get Google to acknowledge, and they fired her instead of acknowledging these problems. So, I think for me as a human and as a writer, I follow very closely what Timnit Gebru is doing and what Dr. Buolamwini is doing, and I think they're actually the ones who are thinking very realistically about ethics and how do you make sure that your data set is bias free. There's a lot of discussion now in the world of AI about how you can take a biased training set and transform it into a model that doesn't exhibit that bias; it's actually called transformer work within AI. Every time someone brings that up, I'm like are you talking about the giant robots from space? And they say, no, we're actually talking about AI.

JFA: Okay.

Annalee Newitz: So, it's a big question, and not surprisingly, I think a lot of the best work in the area is often being done by people who are marginalized in one way or another, so they're aware of what bias looks like. As opposed to kind of just having a theoretical idea of what bias is. And yes, it is the biggest question right now. How do we have ethical AI? And maybe we'll figure it out, or maybe we'll have to take a whole different pathway.

JFA: You made a good point that it's being in the margins that gives the "this is not theoretical; this is real. We have to consider these things because they have happened, and they do happen, and if we don't take care, they are going to happen again. That's a good point. So, I'm looking at the time and feeling like hijacking the whole time, but I won't. But before I open the floor, as people are getting their thoughts together, to start, you know, sharing comments and asking questions, I suppose I would love to ask you to kind of wrap this part up, bearing in mind what is it that you would like to see. And you could take that to fiction; you could take that to the real world. Just what is it that you are really hoping to start seeing?

Annalee Newitz: It's a big question. I really hope that actually in both our storytelling and in our engineering, the work that's being done to develop AI, that we consider what exactly it is that we're trying to model, and if what we're trying to model is the human mind. Then we really need to take seriously the fact that our goal is ultimately to create people. And if our goal is to create people, then we have to think about the kind of care and love that we put into building actual people when we try to raise children, and when we try to educate people. You know, we put, ideally, a lot of thoughtfulness into that, and we also put a lot of boundaries up, like a lot of ethical boundaries, a lot of guidelines for how we treat each other in situations where we are educating someone or rearing someone. And also, thinking about things like civil rights and civil liberties, like what are the rights here in the States, when you have a child or a student and you're bringing them up to be an adult, you're planning for them to have the same rights that you have. And I mean, at least so far, that's how it's going in the United States and it could change. And that's not what we're planning for AI in any way. We're not planning to invest love and care. We're not planning to say, all right, well, when you're eighteen, you're going to start voting. How's that going to go? That's the kind of stuff I think about. I think a lot about the robot civil rights movement and what that's going to look like. I have written about that and I'm sure, you know, I'm not the only one who's thinking along those lines. So, what I really hope is that we slow the fuck down and think about what we're doing in the same way, like I said, you'd think about if you're going to have a kid or teach a class, you'd think about that responsibility. And I just don't think thinking about making money is the same thing as thinking about taking responsibility for a person.

JFA: That was a marvelous answer. Thank you so much. And as you were going, I was thinking of all these things, like, "Oh yeah. My doctoral studies are in education. You can get curriculum instructional studies in education. So that's right." Thank you so much. And it's with deep regret, but also great enthusiasm that I'm going to relinquish my monopoly on you and open to the rest of the room. Would people like to share any comments or questions?

You can raise a hand or put it in chat, or if we stay quiet enough you can even unmute yourself and jump into the fray.

The Bad Pennies: Distinguished Scholar Plenary

Alec Nevala-Lee

THANK YOU, EVERYONE, for turning out, and thank you, VICFA, for inviting me—I hope you'll invite me back again after you hear what I have to say today. A couple of caveats before I start. Number one is that this is very much a work in progress. I hope to expand upon this presentation organically along the way, maybe do a revised version, one of these days. This is an exploration of what I think is an interesting story in the history of science fiction. I do have a content warning, which I don't normally give, but I should say that I refer to instances of child abuse over the course of this presentation. That's not what it's actually about, but it is part of the story, and there is no avoiding it. I don't go into detail, and I'm trying to be mindful of people's responses, but it's something that I have to talk about.

So after seeing the theme for this year's VICFA, I started thinking of stories I could tell that would tie into the themes of AI and automation. I remembered a quote that I like by a guy named Jaron Lanier, who is a Silicon Valley legend, often called "the father of virtual reality." A very interesting guy. He wrote a book a few years ago called *You Are Not a Gadget*. One section that I like

Copyright © 2024, International Association for the Fantastic in the Arts goes like this. Lanier says, "The mere possibility of there being something ineffable about personhood is what drives many technologists to reject the notion of quality. They want to live in an airtight reality that resembles an idealized computer program, in which everything is understood and there are no fundamental mysteries. They recoil from even the hint of a potential zone of mystery or an unresolved seam in one's worldview." And the reason that this quote strikes me as interesting is that I think it actually reflects not just the technologists that Lanier is talking about here but also a theme that I've seen in American science fiction.

I think that it is a central theme, something as central as space flight, let's say. And it's the idea of a science of the mind. So if you go back to what is called the Golden Age of Science Fiction, which is sort of my field of expertise, you see this in stories and editorials and discussions in these magazines. You see the question of, "Can you turn psychology into a science?" A field like engineering, where—if you put something into the mind—you know what you're going to get out. This is a theme that you see in a lot of fiction of this period, and I could have chosen a lot of examples.

But one that I wanted to highlight is in this issue of *Astounding Science Fiction,* the January 1941 issue. This is a letter to the editor that says, "Mathematical psychology may show just exactly why Einstein is Einstein [. . . .] In fact, if we can understand Einstein and Hitler down to the mathematical whys and wherefores, we might try to boost along a few Einsteins and cut down on a few Hitlers, and progress might really get going [. . . .] Signed, Isaac Asimov, Brooklyn, New York." The response is from John W. Campbell, the editor of *Astounding,* who says, "Psychology isn't an exact science—but it can be."

If you read up on *Astounding,* or you know anything about Campbell's career, you know where this ends up. After the war, Campbell partners with another writer named L. Ron Hubbard to produce a mental health therapy called dianetics, which eventually evolves into Scientology. It's an attempt to enact the science fictional dream of a science of the mind in reality—a form of therapy that is designed to turn the subject into an idealized individual called the Clear. This is something you see in stories, but Hubbard and Campbell were trying to do it for real, and they were very mindful of their audience. They were trying to sell this therapy to scientists and to science fiction fans.

If you read the original dianetics article, you see a lot of language drawn from cybernetics and computer science that is really Campbell trying to tailor this material to his readers. Hubbard is not super into it. Later on, the two of them have a falling out, and Hubbard goes off with his followers to found Scientology. He discards a lot of the cybernetic material that Campbell had imposed on him. But the impulse to quantify remained. In the '50s, Hubbard developed something called The Emotional Tone Scale. This is basically an attempt to come up with a numerical scale of emotional states, and he assigned numbers to emotions. You actually still see this used as a diagnostic tool in Scientology today. It runs from death at zero, to fear at one, antagonism at two, all the way up to enthusiasm at four, and forty is "serenity of beingness." But there's this very interesting attempt to be very precise. "Making amends" is zero point three seven five. All these emotions are assigned a number, and the idea of reducing people to numbers, or of reducing human temperament to numbers, is one that you kind of see again and again in science fiction.

I've talked about Hubbard a lot, and I'm not going to refer to him again today, but there's another story that unfolds around the same time that I haven't talked about in public before that I wanted to highlight. This is going to be about a guy named William Herbert Sheldon. Sheldon was born in Rhode Island in 1898. He studied at the University of Chicago, and for most of his life he had two careers. Among certain people, he was best known as a numismatist, as a coin expert. He was the author of books like *Penny Whimsy*, about the American large cents. He was an authority in the field for many years, and he was known for trying to make the study of coins more quantitative. In *Penny Whimsy*, he gives you a quantitative scale for evaluating the condition of rare coins. It's basically a scale that goes from one to seventy. It's called the Sheldon Scale, and it's still the basis for the standard scale used by numismatists today. Sheldon says that this is a scale that is intended to aid those who think quantitatively rather than qualitatively, replacing the qualitative verbal descriptions that coin dealers would use in the past with an apparently more objective numerical scale, which seems like a fairly reasonable thing to do.

But the thing about Sheldon is that for most of his career, numismatics was a sideline. He was primarily a psychologist, and he spent years trying to do for people what he did with coins. In books like *The Varieties of Temperament,* he developed a theory called somatotyping or constitutional psychology, and it's interesting because it starts out by trying to define different personality types based on traits that tend to cluster together. So, "relaxation" and "love of comfort." Or "unrestrained voice" and "need of action when troubled." Or "sociophobia" and "vocal restraint." This is reasonable. It's sort of like a Buzzfeed quiz; it's sort of like, "What type are you?"

What makes Sheldon interesting is that he links it to body type. Some of you may have heard of the concept of the endomorph, which is a person who is physically "soft-rounded"; the mesomorph, who is physically firm and rugged; and the ectomorph who is physically thin and fragile. Some people think that Sheldon was saying, "Well, you're one of these three things." He was actually saying that everyone has elements of each type in them, to different degrees.

He develops this system where he can give each person a three-digit number based on the extent to which you express endomorphic, mesomorphic, or ectomorphic traits. And every type of body is given a rating on a scale from one to seven. For example, here are rating somatotypes that he catalogues. The typical rating for a Phi Beta Kappa is a 225; Superman, he says, would be a 272; and these numbers determine character. You can look at someone's number and draw conclusions about what their personality is likely to be like. For example, mesomorphs are people who have pronounced mesomorphic tendencies he associates with criminality. This was a mainstream idea for a while. The image I have here is actually from *Life* magazine in 1951. For a while, this was a theory that was taken seriously. The thing that I find most interesting is that Sheldon based his research on these somatotypes on photographs, not illustrations. If you look at *The Varieties of Temperament* book, you see nude images of young men that were taken to illustrate different body types, and he also published a book called the *Atlas of Men* that contains hundreds of nude images with the faces and other parts of the body blurred out. In the original version of the slide show, I had a few sample images, but I realized that nobody wants to see that, so I removed those. If you're curious, you can look up *Atlas of Men* online; it's scanned on Archive.org, and there are hundreds of these photos. And the obvious question is, where did he get all these young men to pose for these photographs?

The answer is Harvard. If you're curious about this, I recommend a 1995 article from the *New York Times* called "The Great Ivy League Nude Posture Photo Scandal," which is a very interesting read, as you might guess. It's by the reporter Ron Rosenbaum, who reports that when he was an undergraduate at Yale in the sixties, he actually had this incident where, one day, he was taken into a room and told to remove his clothes. They attached metal pins to his spine, and they took photographs of him, saying that it was for posture correction, and that if the photographs showed poor posture, he would be asked to attend a posture remediation class. But there were all these rumors that these photos were being used for something else. He notes that it was a widespread practice at Ivy League and some Seven Sisters colleges, and he notes celebrities from the mid-nineties who might have had their photos taken in this way, from George Bush to Meryl Streep. And there are all these concerns that maybe there was a deeper story here. Rosenbaum eventually gets a credible lead that they were used by William Sheldon, the guy I mentioned earlier, for his somatotype studies, which is clearly a very interesting allegation. How did Sheldon get access, and how did Sheldon convince the Ivy Leagues to take thousands of nude photographs of students for his research project?

To find out more, he has a source that tells him to call a guy. This is in the mid-nineties, after Sheldon has passed away. But there is a guy named Ellery Lanier, who was one of Sheldon's associates who met him in the late forties, and Lanier is an interesting guy. He was a peripheral figure in science fiction for a long time. He was apparently the fact editor for *Amazing* and *Fantastic* magazines. He was a regular panelist on a radio show hosted by Long John Nebel in New York where Lester del Rey and other science fiction figures appeared, and he wrote articles like "Psychoanalysis by Telepathy," which talks about the possibility that a psychoanalyst may be projecting, literally, his own thoughts and feelings onto the patient.

Anyway, Lanier knew Sheldon. Rosenbaum tapped Lanier to get information about what Sheldon was doing, and Lanier essentially confirms that the story that these photographs are being taken to correct posture was actually a façade, in his words, or a cover-up for what they were really doing, which was to gather research materials for Sheldon's somatotype study. Sheldon either took over existing posture programs at colleges or he would convince the college administrators to start new programs. And he took thousands of these nude photos himself. Lanier, when reached about this, defends it. He says this is a valid science; he says that he is doing measurements of Woody Allen and Mia Farrow to determine the reasons for their divorce, which he attributes to the mismatch in the "time horizon" of the two people involved. Just as a footnote, the Woody Allen/Mia Farrow divorce was not about this. It was about something else entirely, but it's worth noting, in light of what is coming up.

So what happened to Sheldon? The very short version is that his project fell apart when he attempted to follow up his *Atlas of Men* with an *Atlas of Women*, which would contain hundreds of nude photographs of young women taken at the Ivy League and Seven Sisters colleges. People freaked out. Word got around, people found out, and many of these photographs were burned or destroyed. And then that was kind of the end. At least, for this case. But as Rosenbaum pointed out, the dream of reducing human personality to a single number is a recurrent one. We have seen this impulse before, and we will see it again. He points out that it's important for people to be skeptical of what people like this would claim. Which is true.

But what I want to underline here is that Sheldon was seen as credible. He was persuasive, at the time. One of his leading supporters was a man named Earnest Hooton, an ethical anthropologist at Harvard who was an expert on comparative anatomy, and he supported and endorsed Sheldon's work. I found a reference to him in the book *Fads and Fallacies* by Martin Gardner, where he says that Hooton has found correlations with certain kinds of criminality: "Robbers tend to have heavy beards, diffused pigment in the iris, attached ear lobes, and six other body traits." And then Gardner says, "Hooton must not be regarded as a crank, however—his work is too carefully done to fall into that category." So this is Martin Gardner, this is the king of sceptics, and he finds Hooton's work credible. He took him seriously. And the point here is not that Martin Gardner should have known better. The point is that these men were convincing. Sheldon, I should note, was a really good writer. Those books are actually very well written. And he spoke the language that would get results within the closed world of the Ivy Leagues. So he seemed like someone who was serious and should be taken seriously.

That was a façade. Sheldon was not honest. There is a really interesting memoir by one of his former colleagues, Barbara Honeyman Heath, where she says that wherever he found discrepancies between what his theory would say and what the data said, he would just change the data. He would change the numbers to fit his equations or his tables. Occasionally, he would physically trim photographs to make them line up better with the idealized somatotype that they were supposed to illustrate. So he was intellectually dishonest. He falsified data to fit the formula. And again, you might say, "Well, obviously this approach is problematic when it comes to trying to talk about human personality or human beings."

But some of his ideas were also wrong when it came to coins. You might think that the coins would be more amenable to this kind of approach, but one of his collaborators, Walter Breen, says that this formula that he used to estimate cent values was wrong, as early as the mid-fifties. It wouldn't work in practice. The reason is that, just like with human personality, the value of a coin is subjective. It's very hard to reduce these things to a science or to a reliable system. And the punchline is that Sheldon wasn't just intellectually dishonest. He was just dishonest, period. He was a coin collector, not surprisingly, and during his lifetime he had access to the collection of the American Numismatic Society in New York, which was near his house, and eventually people started to realize that there were some discrepancies between the descriptions of these coins and the actual coins that were in the collection. They realized that, for years, Sheldon had been swapping them out. He'd been taking inferior samples from his collection and switching them with the better versions in the ANS collection. He did this for one hundred plus coins. So he stole from the Society that he was supposed to be consulting for. And he did this for at least four other collections. He did this repeatedly. He was a serial thief, and he did this—the irony is right there, but I'll take it—while publishing research trying to identify criminals as certain body types. The entire time, Sheldon was clearly not someone who felt bound by the rules of ethical behavior.

If this were all that there was to the story, I think it's still worth sharing. But this is actually where it starts to get really weird. Give me one second, and I'll expand on what I mean, here. So buckle up.

The next chapter in the story is about a guy named Jack Sarfatti. Sarfatti is still around. He is a physicist whom I would best describe as a member of the Esalen crowd of the seventies. If you've ever seen books like *The Tao of Physics* or *The Dancing Wu Li Masters,* he was part of that circle. Today, he is best known for his association with Uri Geller, the Israeli psychic, and for his interest in subjects like ESP and remote viewing.

When I was doing research into Sheldon, I got an interview from 2010 with Jack Sarfatti, where he says that he "was part of a group of super kids, these genius kids that were being studied at the Columbia University Laboratory of William Sheldon, and one of his assistants, a Walter Breen." He says that Alan Greenspan was part of this group before he was; it all had to do with Ayn Rand and the government, Sandia Labs, and he says that the super kids were being tested. They were trying to induce powers in them like telepathy, ESP, psychokinesis, trying to get them to move objects. It never actually worked, but they tried. He says they talked about aliens and flying saucers. And he says, "Oh, and I met Isaac Asimov at that time." And the interviewer says, "When you were part of this program?" And Sarfatti says, "Yeah, they used to take us to all these sci-fi conventions. Walter [Breen] was very much part of the sci-fi scene then, and also he's one of the founders of MENSA." If you look a little bit deeper, Sarfatti talks in his memoir about being part of a group run by the late Walter Breen and associated with William Sheldon, funded by one of the founders of Texas Instruments, Eugene McDermott.

I'll pause to say that there was clearly a conspiracy theory angle here that I don't want to explore, because it's a little messy. I'm trying to just figure out in general what Sarfatti is describing. So let's take a look at an account that appears in a revised version of his memoir, where he says that the kids in the program were tested for ESP. He claims that Breen was "talent spotting" for a project organized by William Sheldon, who advocated a theory of genetic destiny that his critics regarded as little more than repackaged eugenics, and that Walter Breen referred to the group as "mutants": "He might have been only partly joking: to him they represented a new type of human." I emailed Sarfatti to ask him more about this, and he confirmed certain details. He said that these meetings took place between 1953 and I think '56, that the kids involved were given IQ tests, and that they usually met at Walter Breen's apartment. They never met Sheldon. So I have to underline the possibility here that Sheldon either was not involved at all, or he was involved only peripherally in what was really Walter Breen's project.

I'm not going to really go into Sarfatti's larger claims. But I will say that certain details check out. For example, Eugene McDermott, who was one of the founders of Texas Instruments, really did underwrite a lot of Sheldon's research, as part of a group called the Biological Humanics Foundation, and all of the other names and people mentioned in Sarfatti's recollections seem accurate. Obviously, other details are harder to confirm. But there is one source of corroboration that I found. There is a 1954 novel by a guy named Wilson Tucker, a.k.a. Bob Tucker, who was a prominent fan and writer for that period. The book is called *Wild Talent*. And it's a novel. It's a thriller about a telepath who is discovered by the government and then used as a remote-viewing spy for espionage, and it ends badly, as you can probably guess. But the main character is named Paul Breen, and it notes that Paul has "a special faculty" that other people don't have: telepathy. At one point, Paul Breen talks to his government handler, who says, "I am afraid the earth is about to witness still another struggle between the old and the new, between common man and advanced man," and raises the possibility that Paul is not the only one. And then he says that the government is looking for people like this, looking at people who've been processed by the army, and looking at "every single record, every rating and every intelligence test,'" because "if we find one more like you it will be well worth it."

So Paul Breen shares his last name with Walter Breen, who is the person that Sarfatti names as the head of the super kids experiments. And the question is, does this mean anything? Is it meaningful that Tucker uses Breen's last name for a character in his book? And it turns out there is actually a word for when an author—especially a science fiction author—uses a real person's name as an in-joke. It's called Tuckerization, and it's named after Wilson Tucker. This "is the act of using a person's name [and sometimes other characteristics] in an original story as an in-joke." So I can safely say that if Wilson Tucker named a character "Breen," it probably means something.

Which brings us to Walter Breen. I apologize in advance to anyone who knows where the story is going because there are certain things I can't avoid talking about, but it is all for, I think, a good reason. So Walter Breen—and, again, this is the man who Jack Sarfatti said was running William Sheldon's work with super kids—was born in 1928. It's fair to call Breen a polymath. He was incredibly bright, involved in many fields, primarily in numismatics, in coins, and this is how he first met Sheldon in 1950. So Sheldon takes Breen on as his mentor. Breen is also mentored by another numismatist named John J. Ford, and I'd recommend you look him up. He's another kind of shady figure who I think is typical of some of the people in these circles.

Breen expands on Sheldon's work on coins. This is enormously important work in numismatics. If you look in *Coin Collecting for Dummies*, you can still see the Sheldon/Breen Rarity Scale, which is used by collectors. The question, obviously, is how much was Breen involved in Sheldon's other work, like the somatotyping studies? As far as I can tell, he was not directly involved, but they did share certain interests. Breen does say at one point in one of his fanzines that he has "taken part in experiments described by the American Society for Psychical Research as 'impeccable,' which will be written up elsewhere." I've not found that anywhere. I should note that Ellery Lanier, Sheldon's other associate, also reports having to take part in ESP experiments. So there is something going on. I don't know what it was. I don't know if there was a government connection. I kind of doubt that, but there it is. And there is no question that Breen had interest in quantifying human personality, especially genius.

This is an article from the U.P. from 1957 about a "Lonely Genius Club" that Breen founded: young men, mostly, looking for genius women who were "willing to wed and produce future generations of geniuses." Essentially Breen claims he "can spot a fellow genius through several hours' talk and a 14-page test he designed for the purpose." Breen aims to campaign for a special school for geniuses, and he says, "It would be a personal tragedy for us both if I married a non-genius." So, if you're a self-proclaimed genius in the late fifties, early sixties, what do you do? Well, Walter Breen becomes very active in science fiction fandom, and he joins MENSA, although he was not a founder, as Sarfatti implies. I think at best he was one of the first two hundred members of American MENSA. And in 1962, he met Marion Z. Bradley, and they were married in 1964.

So Walter Breen was married to Marion Zimmer Bradley, the author of *Mists of Avalon* and many other famous fantasy novels. And some of you know what comes next. I'm going to be as tactful here as I can. Walter Breen abused children. This is a fact that I think has been proven beyond any reasonable doubt. It was widely known in science fiction circles at least by the early sixties, especially in the Bay Area. It led to an incident that you may have heard of called the Breendoggle, which was the debate over whether to ban Walter Breen from the 1964 World Con in Oakland. Eventually the committee did rule to ban Walter Breen. What I have here is a statement from Alva Rogers, a very prominent fan. I've redacted parts of it that I think are disturbing that I think don't have any relevance to this talk. But I wanted to highlight the idea that Rogers felt that Breen was "confident of the limitlessness of fannish tolerance." He felt that this was a world in which his behavior would be tolerated.

The committee at Pacificon said, "No, this is not okay. You can't be trusted. We are not going to allow you in the convention." And this decision was incredibly controversial in ways that I think are hard to understand today. I won't go into details here, but if you want to look up the Breendoggle, there's plenty of documentation about what happened there. But I would say that the people who defended Breen at the time, many of them said things that I suspect they wish they could take back. I do want to highlight a couple of things that fans were saying at the time. This is a third-person account by Bill Donaho, so make of that what you will, but some people were saying, "Well, we're all kooks. Walter is just a little kookier than the rest of us. Where will it all end if we start rejecting people because they are kooky?" And then other people were saying, "Well, many of us like Marion Zimmer Bradley, and all this is not a very nice welcome to Berkeley for her" and that it might strain relations with her Berkeley fans. So no one comes out of this looking all that great. It's an example of how science fiction, maybe like the Ivy League, is a closed world. It's a world within itself that occasionally loses perspective. I think that's fair to say. I'm not going to dwell on the Breendoggle material, but I do want to highlight a line from William Patterson's biography of Robert A. Heinlein, where he notes that Heinlein and Marion Zimmer Bradley were correspondents. In one letter from around this time, Heinlein writes to her, saying, "The fan nuisance we were subjected to was nothing like as nasty as the horrible things that were done to you two." So he was clearly on her side. It's not clear how much he knew. I will give him that. But there is no question these allegations were true.

In 1991, Breen was arrested for similar offenses. He pleaded no contest and was sentenced to ten years. He died in prison in 1993. And what I want to highlight here is that the reaction from the numismatic community was very similar to the reaction within science fiction years earlier. One person says, "I'm shocked to hear about this. There is still a great mind there." And someone else says, "A terrible shame that all of his research and writing will be overshadowed by this." And there is a really good account of what happened online that says, "it was like the sci-fi dustups of the 1960s all over again. This time, however, it was coin collectors and fans of Breen's numismatic work that came to his defense" (Morgan and Walker).

So these are separate worlds. There is some overlap, but primarily you have the science fiction fans over here, and you have the numismatic community over here, and these are siloed—they are apart. So the revelations that shocked some people in science fiction in the sixties were equally shocking to people in the numismatic community in the early nineties who had not heard about the Breendoggle. And so these worlds were separate, and able to keep the Breen story within that world, until 2014. Some of you might remember this.

In 2014, Breen and Bradley's daughter sent an email that was shared on an author's blog, accusing not just Walter Breen of abuse but also Marion Zimmer Bradley. Almost overnight, it became common knowledge, within fandom. These were allegations that were known, in some form, for years. This was not information that was not publicly available. But it took this blog post for it to gain some kind of virality and for it to spread. And the question is, What happened? Why did it become commonly known in this case but not in the several occasions when this had come up before? The obvious answer is the internet. Information spread very quickly outside those closed worlds before anyone could contain it.

I think that's true. That's an obvious point.

But there is a more subtle point here that I want to make. I want to bring things back to L. Ron Hubbard and Scientology. When we have a closed world of people who think that they are objectively smarter than others, and combine that with the impulse to reduce human behavior and human value to a number, to something that can be quantified, monstrous things can happen. And the effect is what? I would say, on one level, any attempt to quantify things like personality leads to intellectual dishonesty, which obviously goes along with other kinds of dishonesty. I also think that quantifying human behavior runs the risk of dehumanizing others who rank below you on whatever scale you decide to use, whether they're inside or outside the world that you belong to.

There's an example from the news that comes to mind. This is Sam Bankman-Fried, the founder of FTX, the crypto-currency exchange, who was convicted of seven counts of fraud and conspiracy last week. I'm not an expert on Sam Bankman-Fried, but there is a *New York Times* piece about him that said that SBF would submit "the prospect of an interaction with another person to a cost-benefit calculation," and sometimes he would cancel business meetings at the last minute because "he had done some math in his head that proved that you weren't worth the time." At the same time, SBF was "also an avowed hater of Shakespeare," whom he accused of having "one-dimensional characters," "illogical plots," and "obvious endings." My reading here is that this is a person who wanted to quantify the most basic human interactions, while also rejecting Shakespeare, who by most measures is the most advanced attempt we have to deal with human personality in a qualitative way. SBF had a closed world in which he could do this, and he tied it into doing whatever he wanted with other people's money. It worked until it didn't, just as it did with Sheldon and with Walter Breen.

So I started this talk with a quote from Jaron Lanier, *You Are Not a Gadget,* which is a very good book. And I want to close with the full version of the quote that I began with. So, Lanier says, "There are at least two ways to believe in the idea of quality. You can believe there is something ineffable going on within the human mind, or you can believe we just don't understand what quality in a mind is yet, even though we might someday. Either one of these opinions allows one to distinguish quantity and quality. In order to confuse quantity and quality, you have to reject both possibilities [. . .] This desire for absolute order usually leads to tears in human affairs, so there is a historical reason to distrust it." I think this last sentence is true. I've tried to give some examples of this. I think Jaron Lanier understands this pretty well, too. Remember Ellery Lanier, the associate of William Sheldon who told Rosenbaum about the Ivy League scandal? He is Jaron Lanier's father.

"Ways to Freedom": Plenary Interview with Martha Wells, Guest of Honor

Martha Wells, interviewed by Alexis Brooks de Vita

THANK YOU. Martha, you've written so many highly impactful works that are so incredibly innovative in different areas. And I guess I'll start with the example of course of Murderbot, which is how many people know you, though you've just published *Witch King*. So, I'd say, can you just talk with us a bit about inspiration, about the nuts and bolts. For those who don't know, Murderbot is a self-assigned name of an artificial intelligence, a created intelligence, who manages to subvert its own programming and make independent, ethical decisions. So, Martha.

Martha Wells: Well, first, thank you so much. That's really nice to hear, that it's been impactful. My inspiration for Murderbot, I actually had written it in 2016 when it looked like Trump was coming to office. We were starting to sort of really understand that that was a real possibility. My nephew, my niece-in-law, my whole family was basically panicking, and I was panicking and also just absolutely furious. So, I just really needed a place to put that fury. I'd been writing the last book of my fantasy series, The Books of the Raksura, *The Harbors of the Sun*, and I'd just finished the last draft of that. That was not a good place for that fury because it was meant to be a wrap-up for the series. I wanted it to be very satisfying for the readers and give them a feeling of completion. So, a lot of it was characters kind of repairing relationships in the emotional arcs. And a lot of the battles were mostly about freeing people and reconciliation more for these, they're non-human characters, but for their part of their world. So that just wasn't a good place for me being incredibly furiously angry.

And so I got the idea for a Murderbot, you know, out of the blue and realized it was going to be a science fiction story, not a fantasy story because that would fit it so much better, and just a character who was—I don't like writing characters that are victims who can't help themselves because that just is too intense for me. I don't like to read it, and I don't like to write it because I just don't like to inhabit that place because it's a place too many people inhabit, and I've inhabited, and I don't want to do it anymore. So, I wanted Murderbot to be a very powerful character that was constrained basically by the world it found itself in but was also finding ways to freedom through all that, and to making emotional connections and that kind of thing, but also, I just wanted a powerful character that could fight back. And could protect people that it wanted to protect, and that's really where Murderbot came from.

JFA: I apologize. I didn't realize you would stop right there because what I'm hearing is yes, this incredibly powerful character, and we do understand that the social times, right, create the need for the fiction that can speak to us. And I do think that Murderbot exploded in popularity also because so many of us could understand that our potential was suffocated.

Martha Wells: Yeah.

JFA: Talk a bit about that mechanism because actually, in reading it, it's ingenious. Here is a created, thinking entity that understands its creation. We have gone beyond, you know, Frankenstein and desperate need and helplessness. It's independent. It just wants to watch its soap operas. Talk with us a bit more about the complexities of characterization because you did not seem, you as the author, as the creator, did not seem constrained by conventions about artificial intelligence in the creation of this character.

Martha Wells: Okay, yeah, I think that it goes back to, basically, when I first started writing. I was writing secondary world fantasy that was very closely based on historical time periods even though it wasn't set on Earth. But I was very constrained as a person and as an author, and I really had to work to get my emotional beats for the characters because it almost felt like having a character reveal what they were really feeling about something was me revealing it.

And it was too close. There was something I had a kind of mental block that I realized was there, and I was trying to work on. It's taken me a long time and writing fan fiction was an important part of that because with fan fiction the stakes are much lower. You're writing for a small group of people, relatively small compared to a science fiction/fantasy audience. And there's an assumption that this is just for fun. It's your id. You can do that if you want; you can do something more constrained; but you can do anything you want, and I was learning how to express myself. You know, that helped, too, and also just pushing myself on my science fiction and fantasy, to make it get those emotional beats in, and to get closer to the characters. It would feel like there was a wall between me and the characters.

And when I finally got the Murderbot and got the idea for it and started working on it, it was more like I had finally broken through. I so needed to express myself in a way that wasn't beating my head against the wall or breaking something. This is what I needed to do, and so I think that I put a lot of myself into the character, and literally, when you go through every time

Murderbot's annoyed at something, it's generally something I'm also annoyed about. It's somehow based on my real life.

So that, I think, was why so many people identify with it in different ways. I'm putting a lot of myself into it. I'm putting a lot of my struggles with anxiety and depression and the fact that, since I was a kid, I have seen books and TV and movies as a place to retreat to and feel safe. I think that being very specific about my feelings through Murderbot's feelings and really, really trying to get to the root of what, of how it would be experiencing this world and its situation, being very specific allows people to identify with it. Because there was an idea from a while back, and I can't remember where I read about this, it's been so long, that making a character very general, like the sort of generic White guy character that ends up being the hero in a lot of stuff is more identifiable because it's so generic, and it's like that's the opposite of what's true. What we know now is that the more specific someone's character is about their emotions and their reactions to things, the more anybody can identify with that because our basic emotions and basic reactions, even if you aren't from that person's culture, and you're not or you have not been in that situation, you've had that feeling somewhere in your life, even if it was about something else. And so, you can point to it and say, yeah, I know, yeah. That's how I felt when this happened to me. It may be a completely different thing, but that's how you felt. And you know, that's really the root of our connection with each other; we can't live each other's lives or experiences, but all humans are subject to anxiety. All humans are subject to depression, and, you know, feel like they don't matter and that they can't affect anything, and react to that. We all have these same reactions. So, I think that's why Murderbot has been—people feel they can connect to it because when it explains what it's feeling, when it tells them what it's feeling, it's like you identify with that, in whatever way.

JFA: So, that is absolutely true, and I was just taking some notes because our Guests of Honor, our Distinguished Scholars have said, I think, some very thought-provoking things that we need to put more focus on. So, I'm going to give you a few of those.

[Alarm rings.]

Martha Wells: Sorry.

JFA: Okay, so no, it's us, we're glad to have you here.

Martha Wells: That was actually my alarm to get ready to be here.

JFA: Okay. Get ready! Thank you for throwing everything aside and coming right over. So, one thing I'm thinking, I took so many notes, and I guess I do want to know because you do have so many fans here. What impact did fan fiction have? How did that work with your writing? What process was that?

Martha Wells: Oh, okay, I don't read fan fiction of my own work, the stuff that I'm actually still working on, but I wrote fan fiction for *Star Wars* when I was in college and quite a bit of other stuff, you know. Just all kinds of stuff basically and just being able to—I've made some of my longest, closest friends through fan fiction, people I met either through a mailing list or at a fanfic convention. There's a creative freedom in that because you can come up with whatever crazy stuff you want to come up with and talk about it and in a way that's serious, you know.

You can do that with science fiction and fantasy too, but again, I think that because it's not something you're putting your name on, out into the real world, basically. Even if fan fiction is widely read, it's still more of a mostly personal thing between you and the other readers. So yeah, just doing *Star Wars* and I did some *Stargate* and *Marvel* a little bit, and those kinds of things just over the years. And I think that helped me creatively because a large part of fan fiction is taking the canon and saying, "Well, what if this happened instead?" making it more cathartic in a lot of ways. What if everybody died? We can be sad about that. But in the back of our mind, we know that didn't really happen because it didn't happen in the book or the show or whatever but now you can be sad about it and feel cathartic and, "This is how sad I would have been about this if it actually happened, but it didn't." Which is a safe way to, again, it's like—I met someone at a lecture series at Cushing Library one time, and he was worried about his nieces and nephews and cousins because they were all reading this post-apocalyptic YA, which I think *Hunger Games* was coming out at that point, and he was very worried about it because it's like: "This stuff is dark!" and I was like, "Yeah; when I was a kid, I did the same exact thing." I can't read it now because just things particularly like Hurricane Katrina and Hurricane Ike being so close to where I live really impacted me in a lot of ways, and seeing how many people suffered from that, I just can't read post-apocalyptic, anymore. It's just like I've seen too much of what that might look like, and it's like I can't; it's too close. But when I was a kid, I used to read it all the time because that's how kids learn how to process big things like that. Like children's books: my children's books are about death and everything; it's because the kids need to learn how to deal with that so it's not this big, giant, scary thing, and especially the post-apocalypse stories where you see people, particularly kids, surviving it. And that's important. So, fan fiction and emotional—fan fiction's got some elements of that in it, too. There's a lot of people writing fan fiction to process. Not just for fun but also to process things that they are trying to deal with, which can also be fun if you do it, you know, in a way where you feel really free about it, I think.

JFA: So, I think that your own engagement with writing fan fiction, you mentioned *Star Wars*, you mentioned *Stargate* and trying to make it turn out the way it should have gone. I think that that comes across in your writing now. Because you did something and in fact another one of our guests in his interview, Steven Barnes, did talk about something that I've continued to think about, and he talked about, you know, challenging himself to really get into the story, make it real, make it believable, of course, which is a strength of yours, as well. And he talked about then getting to the penumbral place, right? Here's the sunshine. All right, this is exciting. I'm inspired. I'm going to do this; and inevitably, there is the penumbra, the darkness, and the cold, and the solitude, the isolation.

And anyone who consumes your work, you know, we can put our faith in you. You're going to drag us out of the darkness. We don't know how. But we know that you are the other, and I saw here; I took notes. You mentioned anxiety. You mentioned depression, and you have this incredibly believable character. I'm focusing on the Murderbot because the topic is AI, but that is in fact suffering from post-traumatic stress disorder and has named itself after the unspeakable action it once took. And that engagement is so real. How do you deal with that penumbral stage: your own, the character's, the process's, whatever you're willing to talk to us about?

Martha Wells: Yeah, I think me writing things like this is my way of dealing with it. In some ways, it's always been, I think. I went from dealing with it through reading and watching TV and movies, reading books and watching TV and movies through trying to write things that were more specific to me. It kind of surprised me about the PTSD because I've had people tell me Murderbot felt very realistic for that. You've had influences, particularly when you're really young, you forget about until something reminds you of them. I realized one of my big influences was my father who was a World War II veteran who'd been in a Nazi prison camp. He'd been wounded through the ankle, shot through the ankle, and he still had that wound. I mean years later, when I was a kid, and that's my first time I actually realized that happens: people can get an injury like that and it will still reopen, and it just won't heal up, you know. This is a really terrible thing, and later you know, with lots of hindsight I can see that he had untreated PTSD because they just didn't know as much about it then. And the problem with someone who has untreated PTSD is they can't communicate it to other people because of just not being able to deal with it. And this was mostly emotional abuse and things like that. So. Yeah, I think I've been trying to deal with that through different characters for a long time. And Murderbot, I think is where I really put enough of myself on the page, I think, for Murderbot, that that started to show, probably, enough for people to maybe recognize it more.

JFA: In fact, when I was talking actually with Steven Barnes and he brought up this issue, you know, getting through the darkness and feeling the aloneness, and having gotten to the depths of the problem, right, and then the need to come back out, I actually was thinking when you started talking about Murderbot, and I know that others have said that here's an AI suffering from PTSD, and it's a fascinating concept. But this is then the question. Because what you're describing, I mean, I'm very sorry about your father, and I sympathize; I had my mother, my father, some uncles who were in military service, and the scars are very real. And I think that there is a correlation there because the sense of a governmental parental figure, the overwhelming sense of power and that this trusted entity that is supposed to house and protect you, sent you in there. And I do think that these huge concepts we're dealing with come through this character. But it's always empowering, so I do want you to talk with us a bit about that vision. You're breaking barriers and we're going to get to that. But I do want us to talk about what you're thinking that makes you just keep knocking down these conceptual barriers.

Martha Wells: I don't really know. I just don't know. I think it's had a lot to do with my own issues; it's just the stuff I come up with that I want to write. And I don't always know. I come up with a lot of ideas, and I don't always know which one I'm going to be able to really get into because sometimes I'll start something, and I'll just be bored by it and and have to stop it. My agent has a problem with this too because every time we discuss where I'm going with my career, and I'll go off and do something different. So, we just gave up on trying to plan for me. So, I think that probably a lot of my—oh, I'm not answering your questions exactly—but my motivations have to do with dealing with powerlessness. Having felt powerless for a lot of my life and stuff as a kid, growing up. Also, the lack of trust. Because being emotionally abused by a parental figure, you know, leads to a lot of automatic distrust because you had someone who's supposed to— again like exactly like you said, this thing that's supposed to take care of you did not. And, trying to deal with that, and also trying to—I think in my life I've kind of found my way out, and it's in my writing I seem to be doing a lot of retracing that path. For my characters. Is that what you were getting to, at the root of your question?

JFA: Definitely, Martha, and I should have told you first of all a disclaimer. I mean, I'm going to ask you questions. I'm really thrilled to be able to talk to you. But whatever it is that my questions inspire you to explain, it's actually, you know, the floor is yours.

Martha Wells: Okay.

JFA: And so I want you to just, you know, free flow, whatever it makes you think of. Because I think that what you're touching on is there are few things that I feel safe saying are universal, but I do think we're in literally a worldwide time of universal feelings of discouragement and loss. The world has been pushed, you know, to limits we never imagined, and we can only hope are these the limits? Have we gotten there yet? And the terror is, I guess, it's kind of shocking. But it continues day by day.

Martha Wells: Yeah.

JFA: And so here comes another question that you can handle any way you want to. And that question is, I've been struck in visiting different conversations, different readings, about the very different conceptions of AI: artificial intelligence and automata and the place of art in interactions with, you know, algorithmic calculation, I guess I'll say. And here is something that I think, again, you have mastered, and so I'll put it like this. In a conversation with Wole Talabi, and I'm now mixing it with listening to Jennifer Rhee, the concept has been made clear to me that to take what we've seen of AI so far and assume that that is all it can be, it can only be programmed to hold up a hegemonic structure, is limiting our own thinking, our own concepts, our own creativity, and our own ability to envision a future. Right? It's here, but it's not predetermined. Can you talk and, yes, this is where my previous question was going, can you talk with us a bit about imagining the AI, the automata, about the use of algorithms, about the interaction, the interface with art, please.

Martha Wells: Yeah, I agree about the idea that right now when the AI that's been developed recently like Chat GPT and that kind of thing, there seems to be only one path for it, and that's for corporate aggrandizement, you know. And yeah, and I think it is important for us to try to think about what an AI like that could be used to help people, to actually do good as opposed to, you know, destroy the whole history of art all over the world, basically, is what it's trying to do now. And just for someone's profit, basically.

I put a real delineator between the algorithms we have now like Chat GPT and the idea of true sentient AI, which we don't have, you know, AI that can think for itself as opposed to—gosh, I don't know if it was in this conference—someone had described it as, I think it was Annalee Newitz who described it as like a piece of a mind that's pulled out of the rest of the mind and just is forced to operate under such a limited circumstance, and that's more what we have now as opposed to an actual thinking being that's making its own decisions. I saw a show just last night that I wanted to like, but it had that, "Oh in two years, you know, we'll all be killed by AI, the singularity." I don't know why it's so many things want you to believe that right now. It feels very like people trying to convince you of something that's not good for you. I can't remember the word for that, but yeah.

So, I don't think I know enough about how algorithms work to really come up with ways that you could take like that kind of Chat GPT thing and use it for good. I'm sure there's ways to do it if you could abstract that from the corporations that control it, basically, as opposed to sentient AI where I think it's easier to imagine a thinking being, you know, who's not human and so has different agendas, different priorities and different wants and needs. And I think part of that has been for me is because, when I grew up, there was a lot of, "Oh, the evil supercomputer we created is going to take over the world" kind of stuff, and Ann Leckie and others have talked about how that's really an analogy for a justification for slavery: "Well, we created this sentient being and it's evil. So, we're justified in whatever we do to keep it under control because otherwise it will kill us." And hell, that's like the first, that's Rossum's Universal Robots, basically. That's the plot that kind of repeats through our literary culture about AI. And just taking the idea that like Murderbot—part of the idea for Murderbot is what would an AI really want? Maybe it would just want to be left alone. What would you do if you could be left alone and just do whatever you want? I'd just watch TV and just do that kind of thing.

It's 2016, and the political landscape is horrifying, and I just would really like to retire somewhere where I don't have to think about anything except, what stories I can just pull around myself like a big old blanket. So yeah, so that's really more what I've been exploring, and I'd be interested to read stories like the others are talking about with taking these algorithms and using them for good, basically, for supporting humanity in different ways as opposed to controlling our imagination. Actually, there was a while back maybe in 2017, 2018, I think, I did a very short Murderbot story as part of a thing for *Wired* where they were doing work in the future, and someone, now I can't remember their name, did a story about creating an algorithmic AI that was used to keep in an isolated rural area, I think in an island that had been hit by a hurricane. But it was keeping old people who lived alone, keeping them entertained and also giving them someone to talk to, and also watching out for them, monitoring their health, and then when the hurricane comes along, it's cut off from the medical resources it can access, and then when the characters are coming to like look for people, they find that this person it was taking care of has died, and it couldn't do anything about it. And that was just really a good use of an AI, I think, something that will be a bit of a caretaker for someone who can function on their own but still needs help: needs communication and something to keep an eye on them and be able to know when to alert others to come and help them.

JFA: Exactly. I do believe it's, Annalee Newitz who has a short story like that, and I was trying to get the other half of it: "Crow" is in that title. I linked everyone to it at one point. I'll come up with that. And that is, I think, the kind of innovation we want to start helping ourselves think about and address. I'm going to stop giving you my questions because I see the chat's been filling up, and I've been a little bit of a negligent host, so I'm going to try to fix that right now. So here we go. I hope that I did ask you if a recording was okay, and if I didn't, I apologize. I believe we are recording.

Martha Wells: No, yeah, that's fine. That's totally fine.

JFA: Thank you.

Reviews

Ekpeki, Oghenechovwe Donald and Joshua Uchenna Omenga.
  Between Dystopias: The Road to Afropantheology. Caezik SF &
  Fantasy, 2023. ISBN: 9781647100841, US $17.00 (paper)

Gods and ancestors are not dead, resigned to the past and
forgotten, but live among humans and manifest the multifaceted
myriad of realities that they (we) experience. So argue
Oghenechovwe Donald Ekpeki and Joshua Uchenna Omenga in
Between Dystopias: The Road to Afropantheology. They initialize
the eponymous "Afropantheology" as a mode of literary and
cultural production that relates to the fantastic to encapsulate
"primordial African stories inherited from priests and lore keepers
who were in communication with the deities and the spirit world"
(Ekpeki and Omenga 3).

The relationship between fantastical storytelling and
cosmological history is invoked in terms of breaking down the
boundaries—imposed by European colonial thinking in an
Enlightenment tradition—between the everyday historical record
of facts about existence in the physical world and the fantastical
realm of the spiritual as a method for explaining phenomena. As
such, the stories collected within this conceptual framework offer
an alternative to histories of peoples and places othered by
colonialism—"not folklores, but (fictional) renderings of the
histories passed down from keepers of African culture and lores"
(ibid.). Stories that represent the facts of daily interaction between
and among African deities and human persons are thus to be read
not as fantasy or folklore; instead, the authors argue, they are
Afropantheological in scope, arising out of the histories of African
cosmological traditions to explain past and present realities.

The relationship between history and the present manifests through interactions between and among immortal gods and mortal humans and represents the vibrant interconnection between the spiritual realm of deities and ancestors and the physical realm of humans. Thus are worlds made manifest through the inter-relationality of the realms. The authors write: "Every sphere of existence is connected to the other: the living to the dead, the born to the unborn, humans to the deities" (Ekpeki and Omenga 1). The pathmaking intervention of this collection clearly articulates that our world is not governed by spiritual and physical—or technological—forces that are forever separated but instead reminds us that these essential building blocks of worldmaking are always-already intertwined—at least when the world is viewed through an African cosmological lens. Collapsing the divide between physical and spiritual realms to existence provides a powerful space for imaginative storytelling and another way of looking at and explaining experiences of the world around us. *Between Dystopias* provides two important streams—new theoretical and narrative tools and a centering of African and African Diasporic ways of relating—that are on full display in all of the stories and essays in the mixed collection and which push outward and forward the boundaries of research and reading in the cultural production of the fantastic.

The theorization as *Afropantheological* of what might be mislabeled fantasy or fantastical works to right an historical and ongoing wrong and to center African ways of knowing and being. *Between Dystopias* rejects the notion that what has not been considered to be scientific must be magical thinking. In the introduction, the authors declare that, "There are no magics in these stories, except if by magic one means what is not provable by science" (Ekpeki and Omenga 2). Read alongside the important work that the book performs to bring together the worlds of the scientific and the spiritual in the pursuit of representing and explaining everyday phenomena, this overstatement of a simpler truth presents a tautology. If magic serves only to explain otherwise than science of presumably Europe and its Diaspora, how are we to understand African cosmological systems on their own terms as scientific worldmaking in their own right? I suggest instead that the stories and essays restore the relationship between the mythological and the historical to explain how magic and science offer multiple modes of narration to explain how worlds work. As the writers also state, "It does not suffice to merely insist that these stories are the realities of the African cosmology, especially in this era of scepticism when only the scientific is believed to be factual. [... they] are yet not wholly imaginative" (Ekpeki and Omenga 2). What the authors do not directly declare is that the Afropantheological articulates ways of worldmaking that center African Indigenous scientific knowledge.

The stories collected in *Between Dystopias* disrupt the dichotomization of imaginative stories and scientific ways of explaining worldly phenomena. As such, they offer entire systems of knowing and of explaining knowledge formation and transfer, thus presenting a parallel to western scientific understanding that could be considered alongside it. For example, the protagonist Kambili in "A Dance With the Ancestors" loses everything when a regicide replaces the familiar logics of governance with a would-be autocrat who proclaims his pre-eminence. When the community elders—misunderstanding the facts of the situation or ignoring them for socio-political cohesion—proclaim Kambili guilty of the murder, he must find a way to combat lies with truth, such that the community will accept it—and him—as the way forward. The story clarifies that he will not be able to perform this work by relying on the facts of his experience of the world, because the lies told by his opponent offer a compelling alternative story. Kambili must rely on guidance from another plane of existence if he is to find a way to right the wrongs he faces. He calls on communal ancestors, who intervene to restore justice by preventing the true murderer from claiming the throne vacated by his killing of the king. The ancestors perform this work by teaching Kambili, through the intermediary of a kind of shaman called Azini, to see his surroundings in terms other than he has heretofore engaged. He details his transformation as one of phenomenological transformation of the senses: "It seemed to him that some strange forces had taken over his senses, so that he could now hold discussion with inhuman beings. He had heard stories of those seduced by strange powers into talking with stones and claims that the stones replied to them" (Ekpeki and Omenga 81). Kambili's ability to speak with more-than-human persons ultimately enables him to overcome the lies of his oppressor and regain what was lost, speaking to the capacity of the spiritual realm to speak truth to power in the physical realm. The story evidences the multilayered knowledges at play in its setting and exemplifies the knowledge systems that the collection advances.

Encounters with ancestors and ancestral knowledge empowers another protagonist in "O2 Arena." The ancestral presence in this story clearly troubles the line between the physical realm of human life and the spiritual realm of ancestors, as characters must exist with one foot in each in order to fully value the meaning of living in their dystopian world. An encounter with the spiritual realm of ancestors transitions the protagonist and their beloved to enable societal change, but the story otherwise progresses in mostly realist: in a fashion that is at least as realist as the science-fictional mode allows.

Rather than playing out in a mythical not-time, as with "A Dance With the Ancestors" and others in the collection, this story more visibly plays out in a near-Earth setting and takes the reader forward to a perhaps not-so-distant dystopian future when the air has been depleted of breathable oxygen and those who are not affluent enough to purchase life-saving technology outright must literally fight for breath. The story manifests the metaphor and offer literal state of not being able to breathe due to the oppression of a regime of power that refuses the basic rights of the persons under its yoke. It is possible, for example, to hear while reading "O2 Arena" the dying call of Eric Garner as he was choked to death by police officers in New York City or of George Floyd, similarly murdered by police in Minneapolis. This is certainly part of the story's paratext, which remembers these voices as it centers others who are dying to breathe yet desire to live; in this sense the story also frames a larger understanding of the climate of dehumanizing destruction to which extrajudicial killings contribute, alongside the disproportionate death toll of the COVID-19 pandemic and the overarching environmental disaster—and other world-ending violence. The positioning of the climate as one in which human beings cannot easily draw breath without struggle brings forward a larger theoretical understanding of what novelist Ben Okri calls "the apocalypse of human values" and cultural theorist Christina Sharpe refers to as "the weather" of anti-Blackness. This plays out in "O2 Arena" through a literal arena in which those who cannot otherwise afford their supply of air can cage fight to the death for the entertainment of those who fund the winner's lifetime supply of oxygen. One of the contestants will be killed, and the survivor-murderer will be paid out in "what equaled near three decades of standard wages. Fifty thousand O2 credits, a lifetime supply of air. You fought and died to keep breathing" (Ekpeki 130). If one doesn't immediately die, one lives to breathe for a while longer.

Amid this depleted climate in a slowly dying world, all the markers of poor health that readers might recognize from twenty-first century consensus reality are also present in the story, and various illnesses brought on or exacerbated by lack of clean, breathable air persist. The characters centered in the story are among those whose very right to breathe, thus to live, is constantly threatened in this way. When the unnamed protagonist learns that the person they love, Ovoke, has been diagnosed with a terminal illness from which she will not be able to recover without a ready supply of air to breathe, they understand that they will have to fight in the arena to save her life. But "O2 Arena" proves to be a tragic love story. Although the protagonist wins the fight and secures the necessary oxygen supply, they learn that Ovoke has died while they were fighting. Yet death in the Afropantheological mode allows for sorrow at the passing of a loved one and also for the transition through death to a future of one's own making. The transition from terminally ill human to immortal ancestor marks Ovoke as capable of future world-making. Ovoke, once a victim, becomes an agent of change as her death spurs the protagonist to action. They enter the arena and fight to the death, killing their opponent and securing the oxygen that Ovoke would need. Although they initially do not know that this action has come too late, and Ovoke has died during the fight, this, too, serves as a turning point. What has simmered until they learn of Ovoke's death boils over, and the protagonist remakes their life for the purpose of using the oxygen they have won to right the wrongs they see in society. They go on to take down a serial rapist, and the story ends with the suggestion that they will take on the establishment who have monopolized the right to breathe. In a final declaration, they proclaim, "This world, *our* O2 arena, is now open" (Ekpeki 143, emphasis in original). The Afropantheological mode in "O2 Arena" evidences how interactions between the mortal and immortal—or the physical and the spiritual—realms empower normal lives to resonate beyond their circumstances. The continued presence of the protagonist's love for Ovoke turns him toward a different way of relating to his world after her ancestral transformation. The story thus takes on a form familiar from other mythological or fantastical storytelling, while it also centers and cements an African cosmological awareness. It evidences the knowledge of multiple realms of existence as magical and scientific ways of being in and relating with the world.

Reviews often separate the fictional from the academic, but such a distinction proves futile for the work at the center of this study: *Between Dystopias* collects short fiction and essays, and ultimately also articulates and theorizes new tools for research in science / speculative fiction and the fantastic to engage. Yet a remaining and persistent question that troubles my reading here is whether a theorization through essays and short fiction that so clearly separates its traditions from those of fantasy should appear in a journal dedicated to the pursuit of the fantastical. I find space to do so because it is not my understanding that Ekpeki and Omenga intend to forever separate the fantastical from the Afropantheological; rather, in my reading, they argue in favor of reframing the use of terminologies to conflate, relate and relegate cosmological-spiritual and physical aspects of human experience. What might be read as fantasy in one setting can certainly be read otherwise in another, and this provides an important insight. Ekpeki and Omenga—rightly, in my view—assert that the Book of Revelation can be read as fantasy or not; like Revelation, Afropantheological stories

> are fantasy only insofar as the channels of their passage are dismissed, as has unfortunately been done for centuries now, when the continent's jugular was slashed with the swords of slavery and colonialism, and its history and culture and stories poured into the arid sands of theft and erasure. (2)

It falls to academics and creatives alike to understand the interpolation of the realms, especially when handling African cosmological subjects. Rather than a contentious claim regarding the contours of fantasy, this instead becomes a clarion call to go further, proving one of the greatest insights of *Between Dystopias*.

The stories in the collection are, as the writers acknowledge, "imaginative and didactic stories usually involving outlandish creatures and heroes, meant to entertain and sometimes to instruct [...] not folklores but (fictional) renderings of the histories passed down from keepers of African culture" (Omenga and Ekpeki 3). To resolve this tension the authors might more carefully connect the Afropantheological to other literary modes that reconsider the relationship between storytelling and systems of knowing and being in the world. Connections to the wider African Diaspora would be interesting, for example, by thinking with works like Andrea Hairston's "Seven Generations Algorithm" or Dilman Dila's "Red Bati" that also consider the relations among physical and spiritual, humans and ancestors and the spiritual technologies that empower and transform them. In this vein, looking to Nisi Shawl's theorization of the "spiritual technology" of *Ifa* would take the conversation still further and enrich some of its finer points. So, too, would enabling a closer connection with the work of Zhaleh Boyd on "ancestral co-presence," by which Boyd conceptualizes how the transitioned empower the living. Focusing on twenty-first century hashtag activism, Boyd shows that projects such as "#SayHerName" make present those who have been slain as ancestors who empower contemporary movements, and Boyd then develops this, as Ruha Benjamin states, in terms of historical figures "who called upon ancestral powers in their fight against imperialist, white supremacist opponents" (Benjamin 47). One reads here the contours that would more completely theorize how African ancestral co-presence and Afropantheology work together to advance a conceptualization of the impact of these stories to connect past, present and future histories and in terms of the intertwining of spiritual and physical presence.

As a result, more work remains to be done, and it is important that this intervention be carried on. Readers and scholars in areas of Science / Speculative Fiction and Fantasy, African SFF, theology, Afrofuturism, and literature generative of the African Diaspora will all benefit from reading this powerful addition to existing creative and scholarly research.

Works Cited

Boyd, Zhaleh. "1800 and More: Mourning the Needy Dead in the Chaos of the Present." African American Studies Graduate Student Conference, 20 April 2017, Princeton, NJ: Princeton University. Unpublished conference paper.

Benjamin, Ruha. "Black AfterLives Matter: Cultivating Kinfulness as Reproductive Justice." *Making Kin Not Population*, edited by Adele Clarke and Donna J. Haraway, Chicago: Prickly Paradigm, 2018, pp. 41-66.

Ekpeki, Oghenechovwe Donald, and Joshua Uchenna Omenga. *Between Dystopias: The Road to Afropantheology*. Rockville, MD: Caezik SF & Fantasy, 2023.

Dila, Dilman. "Red Bati." *Dominion: An Anthology of Speculative Fiction From Africa and the African Diaspora*, edited by Zelda Knight and Ekpeki Oghenechovwe Donald, Louisville, KY: Aurelia Leo, 2020, pp. 11-19.

Hairston, Andrea. "Seven Generations Algorithm." *Trouble the Waters: Tales From the Deep Blue*, edited by Sheree Renée Thomas, Pan Morrigan, and Troy L. Wiggins, Nashville, TN: Third Man, 2019, pp. 3-29.

Shawl, Nisi. "*Ifa*: Reverence, Science, and Social Technology." *Extrapolation*, vol. 57, no. 1-2, 2016, pp. 221-28.

ANDREW ERICKSON

www.ingramcontent.com/pod-product-compliance
Lightning Source LLC
Chambersburg PA
CBHW011801040426
42449CB00016B/3461

9 781786 958990